Cambridge Elements ≡

Elements in the Renaissance
edited by
John Henderson
*Birkbeck, University of London, and Wolfson College,
University of Cambridge*
Jonathan K. Nelson
Syracuse University Florence

PLAGUE, TOWNS AND MONARCHY IN EARLY MODERN FRANCE

Neil Murphy
Northumbria University

CAMBRIDGE
UNIVERSITY PRESS

Shaftesbury Road, Cambridge CB2 8EA, United Kingdom

One Liberty Plaza, 20th Floor, New York, NY 10006, USA

477 Williamstown Road, Port Melbourne, VIC 3207, Australia

314–321, 3rd Floor, Plot 3, Splendor Forum, Jasola District Centre,
New Delhi – 110025, India

103 Penang Road, #05–06/07, Visioncrest Commercial, Singapore 238467

Cambridge University Press is part of Cambridge University Press & Assessment,
a department of the University of Cambridge.

We share the University's mission to contribute to society through the pursuit of
education, learning and research at the highest international levels of excellence.

www.cambridge.org
Information on this title: www.cambridge.org/9781009507639

DOI: 10.1017/9781009233798

When citing this work, please include a reference to the DOI 10.1017/9781009233798

First published 2024

A catalogue record for this publication is available from the British Library.

ISBN 978-1-009-50763-9 Hardback
ISBN 978-1-009-23378-1 Paperback
ISSN 2631-9101 (online)
ISSN 2631-9098 (print)

Plague, Towns and Monarchy in Early Modern France

Elements in the Renaissance

DOI: 10.1017/9781009233798
First published online: March 2024

Neil Murphy
Northumbria University

Author for correspondence: Neil Murphy, neil.murphy@northumbria.ac.uk

Abstract: This Element examines the emergence of comprehensive plague-management systems in early modern France. While the historiography on plague argues that the plague of Provence in the 1720s represented the development of a new and 'modern' form of public healthcare under the control of the absolutist monarchy, this Element shows that the key elements in this system were established centuries earlier because of the actions of urban governments. The Element moves away from taking a medical focus on plague to examine the institutions that managed disease control in early modern France. In doing so, it seeks to provide a wider context of French plague care to better understand the systems used at Provence in the 1720s. It shows that the French developed a polycentric system of plague care which drew on the input of numerous actors to combat the disease.

Keywords: plague, France, absolutism, monarchy, towns

ISBNs: 9781009507639 (HB), 9781009233781 (PB), 9781009233798 (OC)
ISSNs: 2631-9101 (online), 2631-9098 (print)

Contents

1 Introduction

On 12 August 1720, Philip of Orléans, regent of France, sent the physicians François Chicoyneau and François Verny, along with the surgeon Jean Soulier, to investigate an illness which had irrupted at Marseille. Although they initially supported the town council's insistence that it was not plague, as deaths continued to increase it soon became clear that it was the feared disease.[1] The *conseil d'État* (the principal royal council) issued orders throughout the summer, first restricting contact between Marseille and the rest of Provence, and then, as the disease spread beyond the city, between Provence and the rest of the kingdom. Sanitary cordons were placed around affected communities, most notably the stone wall constructed in Vaucluse, and guarded by soldiers with instructions to shoot anyone who tried to escape. On 5 September, Charles Claude Andrault de Langeron, commander of the king's armies, was dispatched to Marseille to enforce the city's plague regulations and maintain order, while similar military appointments were made at other towns. Royal officials and health boards throughout Provence remained in close contact with Versailles, which organised relief measures for the stricken areas, including the sending of provisions and medical staff. In early 1721, a royal health board (*Conseil de la santé*) was established at Paris. It was composed of the most important men in the royal government and met twice a week to discuss the situation in Provence.[2]

The high level of Crown involvement in the management of the plague of Provence has been seen as the emergence of a new and 'modern' form of disease control. A recent study of the outbreak finds that 'the management of the Provençal plague symbolized a break from the past, marked in part by augmented communication between Crown and provincial officials that represents an early example of the more comprehensive state-centralized responses to disasters that we see all over the globe today'. It was a 'unique' outbreak of plague which 'represented the first, most prominent opportunity to advance the power of the state in the name of public health', and for France 'practices that previously rested in the hands of municipal officials were now controlled and overseen by the central government'.[3] Yet, although the scale on which the royal government operated in the 1720s was certainly extensive, very few of the above-mentioned factors can be considered genuinely new. As we shall see in this Element, there had been significant levels of royal involvement in the management of plague outbreaks in France long before the 1720s. Rather

---

[1] Chicoyneau was an anti-contagionist, which undoubtedly influenced his views here: Jones and Brockliss, *Medical World*, p. 354.

[2] For a good overview of these events, see: Takeda, *Marseille*, chapter 4.

[3] Ermus, *Disaster*, pp. 16, 55, 60 (for broader information on this point, see chapter 1 of that book).

than viewing the plague of Provence as a new form of modern disaster management, we should see it as the fullest expression of a disease-control system which had been developing in France over the previous two and a half centuries.

The special place which the events of the 1720s have assumed not only in the history of France but in the historiography on plague more widely reflects the extensive amount of work on the subject. There are at least a dozen books on the plague of Provence, in addition to numerous journal articles.[4] It is probably the most studied single outbreak of the plague in early modern Europe. Where other European states have seen a flowering of studies in recent years on the management of early modern plague relief, the two centuries preceding Provence are poorly covered in the historiography on plague in France.[5] Yet France was the largest state in western Europe, and it developed a sophisticated system for managing the disease. By the seventeenth century, France had more plague hospitals than any other country, including the largest institution in Europe: the Saint-Louis hospital in Paris.[6] While there are various studies of individual plague outbreaks or specific locations (and frequently both), many of which are a century or more old now, they tend to cover the same ground, and there are few efforts to analyse wider developments occurring across the kingdom over time. Jean-Noël Biraben's two-volume *Les hommes et la peste* (1975) is a notable exception to this trend, though it also focuses heavily on the plague of Provence (especially in volume 1).[7] Biraben's work was a landmark study and it made a major imprint in the historiography of plague, though his conclusions and interpretations are increasingly attracting criticism.[8] Like many other plague historians of that generation, Biraben took a negative view of the measures used to combat plague, seeing them at best as ineffective and often worse than the disease itself. Moreover, Biraben's principal concern was with the demographic and medical impact of plague, and he was not especially interested in examining the institutional development of plague policies in France.

---

[4] See especially: Alezais, *Blocus de Marseille*; Bruni, *Apt malade de la peste*; Buti, *Colère de Dieu*; Buti, *Peste au village*; Carrière, *Ville morte*; Caylux, *Arles et la peste*; Chauvet, *Gévaudan*; Demichel, *Risque*; Ermus, *Disaster*; Gaffarel and Duranty, *Peste de 1720*; Goury, *Peste de 1720*; Praviel, *Belsunce*; Takeda, *Marseille*. See also: Beauvieux, 'Société marseillaise'; Bollet, 'Traitement'; El Hadj, 'Organisation sanitaire'; Hildesheimer, *Bureau de Santé*.

[5] Recent work on early modern France has tended to concentrate on the medical writing about plague rather than on the institutional response to plague. See: Coste, *Représentations*; Jones, *Patterns of Plague*. While these books tend to emphasise continuity in plague tracts, Samuel Cohn has shown that in Italy plague tracts show a developing understanding of the disease: Cohn, *Cultures of Plague*. See also: Aberth, *Medical Response*.

[6] For the Saint-Louis plague hospital, see: Ballon, *Paris*, pp. 166–98. For the establishment of plague hospitals in early modern France, see: Murphy, 'Plague Hospitals'.

[7] Biraben, *Les hommes*.   [8] Alfani, 'Decline of Italy'; Benedictow, 'Biraben', pp. 213–23.

This Element moves away from the medical and socioeconomic focus to examine the institutions that managed disease control in early modern France, from city councils to the monarchy. It seeks to understand who was responsible for emerging anti-plague measures, who was involved in implementing these disease controls and how the administration of this system developed over time. It starts in the late fifteenth century, with the beginnings of comprehensive disease-control methods in France and continues to the late nineteenth century, when the French were still contending with the second pandemic in North Africa. It seeks to provide a wider context of French plague care to better understand the systems used at Provence in the 1720s. It also moves away from the single-city approach, often favoured in studies of plague in France, to take a national perspective, both because there was not a uniform pattern of development across the kingdom and because single-location studies are not helpful in drawing out wider trends in geographically large states. To this end, it looks at scores of settlements, from big cities in the urban heartlands of France to small mountain villages in sparsely populated regions.

One of the problems with emphasising the extent of the monarchy's involvement in the outbreak at Provence is that it creates a false dichotomy between Crown and town, national and local. Françoise Hildesheimer writes that from the late seventeenth century the Crown displaced towns as the management of the disease moved from 'the local to the national level'.[9] It was in the 1720s in particular when plague-control systems shifted from 'isolated islands, cities acting for themselves' to become a national concern under the monarchy.[10] This focus on the actions of the monarchy intersects with a highly negative view of the urban management of plague. Namely, that municipal councils acted selfishly and locally whereas a more dispassionate Crown was concerned with the health of the entire kingdom, an argument which in many ways follows that made by apologists for the absolutist monarchy in the seventeenth and eighteenth centuries. Yet the king was principally concerned not with the health of all his subjects but with those who lived in the major cities which provided the money he needed to fight his wars. The Crown was so extensively involved with the plague outbreak at Marseille in 1720 because of the city's leading role in international commerce.

With its focus on the big cities, the Crown gave little consideration to the frequently severe outbreaks in the countryside, whose residents were often made to suffer to protect the cities. The monarchy's disinterest in rural plague has often been shared by modern historians, who typically find that early modern plague was predominately an urban disease which largely spared

---

[9] Hildesheimer, *Fléaux*, p. 129.   [10] Hildesheimer, *Terreur*, p. 54.

villages. Recently, historians have started to turn their attention to the country-side and have shown that rural plague could be severe. In an influential article, Guido Alfani argues that plague struck Italy more severely than northern Europe because of the 'territorial pervasiveness of the disease'.[11] He writes that 'in the north [of Europe], plagues affected mainly highly urbanized areas, while in the south, they had much greater territorial pervasiveness spreading more effectively to the countryside'.[12] Yet this Element shows that rural plague was extensive and severe in early modern France. Urban governments recog-nised that the countryside was one of the main sources of infection and they took extensive measures to try and prevent it from spreading. The view that the early modern French countryside (and rural northern Europe more widely) was largely free of plague led Alfani to claim that Italy's experience of the disease in the seventeenth century – whereby both cities and the countryside were decimated – was unique in Europe and underpinned the 'Little Divergence', which saw the economic decline of Italy in comparison to northern European states. Given that this assertion is based on the apparent absence of rural plague from northern Europe (and particularly France), this conclusion is questionable.

An examination of rural plague, which was largely missed by Biraben in his influential database of outbreaks, reveals a new picture of plague distribution in early modern France. The map Alfani provides to support his conclusions for Italy (which is based on data from Biraben and others) shows no outbreaks of plague in France outside of the northeast in the period running from 1650 to 1674, and no outbreaks at all in the kingdom from 1675 to 1699. Yet plague was certainly present in the countryside in the 1650s and again in the 1690s, outbreaks which have gone unnoticed probably because they did not decimate big cities. It ravaged villages across the southwest in the early 1690s but did not hit towns such as Auriol or Martigues which implemented their anti-plague controls in response to the situation in the surrounding countryside.[13] In 1694, Pierre Chirac, the University of Montpellier physician who travelled with the army of the Duke of Noailles through western France, carefully diagnosed the various diseases he encountered, such as typhus and smallpox, but which also included an outbreak of plague.[14] Plague was also present at Angers in 1703 and the infected were placed in quarantine, though it remained at a low level and there was no major outbreak.[15] It is not clear why these outbreaks of plague did not significantly affect major urban populations, but it raises the possibility of different strains of plague, some of which were especially deadly but others

---

[11] Alfani, 'Decline of Italy', p. 410.

[12] Alfani, 'Decline of Italy', p. 412. For rural plague, see also: Curtis, 'Plague Mortality'.

[13] Boudet and Grand, *Documents inédits*, pp. 108–9.   [14] Bourru, *Épidémies, 1694.*

[15] David, *Peste à Angers*, p. 46.

much less so. Rather than seeing early modern plague as just an urban disease with only the rare significant outbreak in the countryside – such as that at Eyam in 1665 – perhaps we should look at it as an endemic and rural disease which had massive flare-ups when, possibly severe, strains hit major urban populations (or that by the later seventeenth century urban populations had acquired a degree of immunity after being hit by the successive severe waves of the disease earlier in the century).[16]

In contrast to the monarchy, which is seen as successfully bringing an end to the disease in France, urban governments are often portrayed as having been ineffective or corrupt, allowing plague to infect their towns as a result of negligence and mismanagement. One recent study has written of 'municipalities paralysed by fear at the prospect of economic and social disorders', and that urban governments 'generally delayed' announcing the presence of plague.[17] According to François Lebrun, 'the measures taken selfishly by each town' were 'often decided late and applied sluggishly', a situation which only came to an end when the Crown took over from the late seventeenth century.[18] According to this view, the absolutist monarchy used its extensive powers to force anti-plague measures on towns. For Lebrun, 'it is in the matter of public health that the action of central power [i.e. the monarchy] is, in the last decades of the Ancien Régime, the most resolute and the most effective'.[19] Colin Jones echoed these statements, finding that 'it could well be that dealing successfully with plague was one of the rather few occasions on which the absolutist state assumed powers that really were absolute'.[20] In contrast, this Element shows that the French monarchy sought to work with urban elites rather than against them. Increased Crown intervention did not displace the involvement of urban governments, which remained as important to the operation of plague-relief schemes in the 1720s as they had been in the 1520s. Rather, French monarchs increased the power of town councils during times of plague and provided them with resources to help implement disease relief schemes. This was especially important from the later sixteenth century, when the increased length of plague outbreaks combined with a massive growth in poverty to exhaust municipal budgets. Rather than acting in a heavy-handed manner, the actions of the French monarchy conform more closely with the model put forward by William Beik and others, who argued that absolutism was founded on collaboration between the monarchy and provincial elites, including urban governments.[21]

---

[16] For different strains of plague and immunity, see: Alfani, 'Decline of Italy', pp. 421–3; Cohn, 'Epidemiology', pp. 84–7.

[17] Belmas, 'Catastrophe sanitaire', p. 31.   [18] Lebrun, 'Intervention', p. 45.

[19] Lebrun, 'Intervention', p. 50.   [20] Jones, 'Plague and its Metaphors', p. 116.

[21] Beik, 'Absolutism of Louis XIV'. For collaboration between the absolutist monarchy and provincial elites, see: Beik, *Absolutism and Society*.

The current view of the nature of royal intervention in plague relief in early modern France also misrepresents the complexities of the system and ignores many key players. Rather than taking a binary view of plague relief – by which the monarchy simply displaced urban governments from the late seventeenth century – we should see disease management in France as being polycentric and involving a range of actors. While municipal councils were unquestionably the principal agents for the development of plague-relief systems, polycentricity was integral to the system from the beginning as towns needed support to implement the measures they devised. The people involved in managing plague outbreaks became increasingly diverse during the sixteenth and seventeenth centuries – and remained so during the outbreak at Provence in the 1720s. Local nobles, the clergy, governors, *parlements* as well as a whole range of royal officials (including *baillis*, *prévôts*, *indendants*) came to play important roles in the implementation of anti-plague methods. Each of these individuals or institutions brought specific powers and attributes, which were essential for the successful operation of plague management schemes, from providing men to enforce police ordinances to imposing regulations over wide areas. Yet these players have rarely been studied. Even the actions of the *intendants* (the principal agents of the Crown in the provinces from the mid-seventeenth century), who are one of the few groups whose importance is noted in the wider literature on plague in France, are barely examined in detail. Moreover, the French monarchy was already involved in the local management of plague by the beginning of the sixteenth century, especially in the form of tax remissions and financial support. From the 1570s, the later Valois monarchs took a more active role in anti-plague measures, though it was really the first Bourbon king, Henry IV (reigned 1589–1610), who developed an increasingly interventionist plague policy which his successors continued. Rather than pitting different groups and institutions against each other, plague was a unifier – one of the few in early modern France – which saw different bodies work together to impose a shared set of regulations against a common enemy.

In sum, the origins of plague management schemes in France lay with municipal governments. These developments began in the south of the kingdom in the second half of the fifteenth century, spreading to the north later. Although urban governments were the principal agents in the creation of these measures, they were supported by other groups and individuals. According to Carlo Cipolla, whose work on plague and public health has been especially influential, the early modern clergy consistently opposed the measures contained in plague ordinances. As well as emphasising a division between Church and state, Cipolla took a dismissive view towards early modern anti-plague measures. He wrote that 'the difference between the two positions [i.e. the clergy and state authorities] was not the difference between truth and error, but between two kinds of error – one blindly rooted in ideology, the other derived from inadequate means of observation'.[22] Yet, as we shall see, there was extensive cooperation between the clergy and state authorities (especially municipal councils) in the implementation of public health procedures, while these anti-plague measures achieved some success in the war against the disease.

Beyond the clergy, local agents of royal or ducal authority supported municipal efforts to combat plague. During the sixteenth century, the *parlements* (provincial legislative assemblies) began to take over responsibility for issuing of plague ordinances. They standardised rules and applied them across wider geographical areas. The provincial governors also came to play a role in implementation of plague measures during the sixteenth century. They used their authority as the king's principal representative in the provinces to help enforce plague measures, which during the sixteenth century assumed the character of police ordinances. To this end, soldiers were regularly used to help municipal councils enforce plague-control measures. As well as supporting town councils, by the early seventeenth century the Crown was also using the governors to monitor the implementation of anti-plague measures in affected parts of the kingdom. This formed part of the monarchy's increasing involvement in the management of plague outbreaks during the second half of the sixteenth century. The monarch's ideas about the best way to manage outbreaks were given physical form in construction of the Saint-Louis plague hospital in Paris in the early seventeenth century, with this design then being rolled out across other parts of the kingdom. Throughout the seventeenth century, plague outbreaks were monitored from court and support was sent to affected towns, though by the 1630s the Crown was already threatening to step in and impose direct military rule on places where the plague measures were not being adequately enforced. The basic system used at Marseille in the 1720s was effectively already in place almost a century earlier.

The changing nature of the management of plague-control systems in France intersects with the chronology of epidemics. The most complete database we have remains that compiled by Biraben in the 1970s, which lists outbreaks of plague in places across the kingdom. Even then, the real impact of plague is likely to have been much higher as his coverage of the kingdom is far from complete, especially in rural areas, which he largely ignored. Moreover, Biraben only noted the frequency of an outbreak rather than its severity.[23] Certainly, this is difficult to achieve for France both due to the vast size of the

---

[22] Cipolla, *Faith*, p. 8.

[23] For the problems in using Biraben's database, see: Roosen and Curtis, 'Historical Plague Data'.

country and an absence for much of this period of the types of records which could be used to accurately estimate death rates. It was not until the 1660s that statistical reports (along the lines of English bills of mortality) were compiled, and even then these were limited to particular towns. It is not really until the plague of Provence that we have extensive sets of statistical data which help us see the demographic impact of plague, though further research into local parish and hospital records, where they exist for earlier centuries, may help provide a more comprehensive picture of the situation in France.[24]

Nonetheless, the records of urban governments provide plenty of information about the frequency and duration of plagues. For instance, between the 1480s – when the first plague hospital was founded – and the 1640s – when the last outbreak of plague occurred in the city – Grenoble was hit by sixteen waves of plague, some of which only had a limited impact on the city, while others lasted for years.[25] The duration of a plague was especially important because the longer a plague the greater its effect on urban governments, which had to provide plague care over an extended period of time. The plague which struck Saint-Flour in March 1564 persisted in the town until early 1566 and led to a massive overhaul of the public health system and the care of large numbers of the poor – a process which decimated the city's finances.[26] Occasionally, we have figures of the number of deaths though it is not always clear where this information comes from. For instance, the plagues which struck Grenoble and Saint-Flour in the 1580s were reckoned to have killed two-thirds of the population, while Marseille was believed to have lost 20,000 people in a single year during this outbreak.[27] While these figures may be impressionistic, nonetheless we know that the outbreak of the 1580s was especially nasty. It struck towns for years at a time and massively impacted on civic budgets. Moreover, these death rates correspond to those of the 1720s, where we have accurate information (for instance, 50 per cent of Marseille's population of 100,000 died during the outbreak).[28] In addition, while there are many problems with Biraben's data, it is useful in seeing wider patterns – patterns which correspond to the material contained in municipal records. Biraben's data suggests that there were successive moderately severe outbreaks of plague in France in the late fifteenth and early sixteenth centuries, which was precisely the time when French towns started to implement developed disease-control systems. Furthermore, all these

---

[24] For the extensive statistical data for the plague of Provence, see: Biraben, *Les hommes*, vol. 1, pp. 310–32.

[25] Chavant, *Peste à Grenoble*, p. 13.   [26] Boudet and Grand, *Documents inédits*, pp. 64–81.

[27] Chavant, *Peste à Grenoble*, p. 13; Boudet and Grand, *Documents inédits*, p. 83; Caylux, *Arles et la peste*, p. 44.

[28] Bell, *Plague in the Early Modern World*, p. 26.

sources emphasise that nasty plagues struck France in major and persistent waves in the late sixteenth century and then again in the 1620s–30s. We should also remember that a tally of places is only part of this picture and can hide important and severe manifestations of the diseases, particularly the regional outbreaks which struck northeastern France in the 1660s and then in Provence in the 1720s, which were deadly but did not spread across the entire kingdom, possibly because of the implementation of measures to contain them.

Before moving on to look in detail at the emergence of plague management schemes in France, Section 2 provides an overview of the development of plague regulations in France's neighbours, particularly England, Spain, the Low Countries and Italy. It considers how these schemes emerged and the interplay between different actors, especially municipal governments and central authorities. If we wish to understand better the development of public health systems in early modern Europe, more comparative work cutting across different states is essential. Section 3 moves on to look at municipal governments in France, showing that they were principally responsible for developing comprehensive plague ordinances from the late fifteenth century. It considers how they enforced these rules and shows that towns worked in regional and national networks to coordinate their efforts long before the central state got involved. Cooperation was important and this section also examines relations between different urban groups, especially the clergy, as well as those between municipal governments and surrounding villages. Paying for plague care was a major consideration, particularly as disease-control systems became especially large and sophisticated, and towns had to deal with more severe plagues. This led urban governments to increasingly rely on the support of the Crown and its provincial agents. Focusing on the importance of collaboration, Section 4 moves on to examine the range of other actors who came to play a role in the operation of anti-plague systems in the sixteenth and seventeenth centuries, such as the *parlements* (regional legislative assemblies), which played an early role in coordinating plague measures and imposing them over large areas. They worked with urban governments, lending support when required. The section then shows how the composition of institutions changed over time, becoming increasingly diverse. The Epilogue considers the legacy of the methods that were devised in France in the years after the plague of Provence. Overall, this Element seeks to offer a new and more nuanced view of the operation of plague-relief systems in France and to open new areas for future research.

2 The Emergence of Plague-Control Systems in Western Europe

In the decades following the Black Death, populations across Europe utilised existing sanitary legislation aimed at removing the miasmas believed to cause disease.[29] Prolonged encounters with plague, which kept returning in waves, led to the development of anti-plague legislation based around ideas about contagion. Words such as 'contagion' and 'infection' were employed by municipal councils of the period, though, as John Henderson reminds us, we should not attribute modern definitions to their meaning in the later Middle Ages and Renaissance.[30] However, although they knew nothing of germ theory, by the late fifteenth century urban authorities did use such words to describe the transmission of plague from person to person. A growing acceptance of ideas about contagion came to exist alongside existing traditional theories regarding the role of corrupt air in spreading disease. There was a growing belief in 'contingent contagion' among urban elites during the early decades of the sixteenth century, with some socioeconomic groups (especially the poor) being considered especially susceptible to infection, which they then spread by corrupting the air and environment.

This medical understanding of plague provided the impetus for the creation of legislation and institutions designed to combat plague. These developments occurred first in Italy, which has long been the focus for examinations of the rise of public healthcare in pre-modern Europe. In the late 1970s, Carlo Cipolla could confidently declare that the Italian states 'developed a detailed organization of public health far in advance of the rest of Europe', and that 'health organisations outside of Italy remained at a more primitive level throughout the sixteenth and seventeenth centuries'.[31] Undoubtedly, Italy stood at the forefront of anti-plague measures, with health boards, plague hospitals, quarantine centres and *cordons sanitaire* proliferating there at an early date. Yet other parts of Europe were not so far behind as once believed. We find plague hospitals in Spain from the 1430s and in France from the 1450s (albeit on a temporary basis), while recent research has shown that pest houses were widely used in England from the 1530s.[32] Moreover, John Henderson reminds us that there was great variance in Italy and the advanced measures taken early by states such as Genoa, Milan and Venice, particularly the use of permanent health boards and plague hospitals, were not uniformly found across the Italian states.[33] Furthermore, not all European states adopted this Italian model (or at least not initially). Towns in Spain and the Low Countries, as well as those in northern France, often were less severe in their application of quarantine regulations. This was the case even in

---

[29] Carmichael, 'Plague Legislation'. For the utilisation of pre-Black Death sanitary legislation in towns across Europe, see: Geltner, 'Path to Pistoia'; Geltner, *Roads to Health*; Rawcliffe, *Urban Bodies*; Rawcliffe and Weeda, *Policing*.

[30] Grmek, 'Notions d'infection', pp. 53–70; Henderson, 'Medical and Communal Responses', pp. 139–41; See also: Nutton, 'Seeds of Disease'.

[31] Cipolla, *Faith*, p. 11.   [32] Crawshaw, *Plague Hospitals*, pp. 22–3; Udale, 'Pesthouses'.

[33] Henderson, 'Invisible Enemy', p. 266.

Italy, with Piedmont adopting a different approach from its neighbours.[34] Nonetheless, the classic Italian model, based around the strict enforcement of quarantine measures, was seen by many, including the monarchies of France and England, as the preferred public health system and virtually all European states would eventually adopt these measures.[35]

Italy

The northern Italian states were at the forefront of the development of comprehensive plague-control systems based around ideas about contagion. By the 1370s, the Visconti dukes of Milan were implementing extensive anti-plague practices, which included separating the sick from the healthy; ordering the reporting of all deaths; establishing commissioners to implement health rules; and caring for the poor – measures which would remain fundamental to health-care systems across Europe during the second plague pandemic.[36] Milan, Venice, Siena, Florence, Pavia, Lucca and Cremona all had health boards by 1500, often temporary at first and then becoming permanent.[37] Yet neither Siena nor Rome had permanent health boards by the early seventeenth century, while the kingdom of Naples had an undeveloped health system, which Cipolla terms as being 'characterized by corruption and inefficiency', though recent work has shown that the outbreaks of the 1650s and 1690s were managed well.[38]

No matter whether it was the Venetian republic, ducal Milan or the Grand Duchy of Tuscany, plague-control measures tended to be developed by the central authorities and then imposed across the state, with bodies such as the *Magistrato alla Sanità* in Florence and the *Provveditori alla Sanità* in Venice imposing measures across the rest of the state. Yet not all the Italian states developed along centralised lines. As Sandra Cavallo has shown, in Piedmont the initiative to develop anti-plague measures came from local authorities and a centralised *Magistrato di Sanità*, whose authority encompassed the entire state, did not develop until the 1570s, a century after the first local measures had been taken, a situation similar to that we find for France.[39] While Italy was politically fragmented, the Grand Duchy of Tuscany led an attempt in 1652 to

---

[34] Cavallo, *Charity and Power*, pp. 44–5.

[35] For reasons of space, I must confine this study to England, Italy, Spain and the Low Countries. For central and eastern Europe (including the Ottoman lands), see: Alexander, *Bubonic Plague*; Eckert, *Structure of Plagues*; Varlik, *Plague and Empire*. For Scotland, see: Jillings, *Urban History of Plague*.

[36] Carmichael, 'Contagion Theory', pp. 215–18.

[37] Carmichael, 'Contagion Theory', pp. 219–21.

[38] Cipolla, *Fighting the Plague*, pp. 4–5; Fusco, 'Naples'. For the development of health boards in Italy, see: Cipolla, *Public Health*, pp. 15–66.

[39] Cavallo, *Charity and Power*, pp. 44–57.

coordinate action against the plague. It was intended that Genoa, the Papal States, Naples and Florence would implement a common set of plague regulations, especially based around maritime quarantine. However, the plan was not realised and only Florence and Genoa joined together in 1652, though this fell apart in 1656 when plague infected Genoa.[40]

While Dubrovnik is widely seen as the place where quarantine was first established in 1377, Reggio Emilia may have used similar measures three years earlier. In any case, once adopted these measures were imitated by others.[41] In 1423, Venice established the world's first permanent plague hospital, with a second one opening in 1471. While many of these institutions were large (such as the plague hospital established at Milan in 1488), they could be insufficient to treat all the infected during severe plagues. The massive plague hospital built at Genoa in the early sixteenth century (the largest in Europe until the construction of the Saint-Louis hospital at Paris) was not substantial enough to cope with the number of people in the devastating plague of 1656–7. Those sent to plague hospitals were segregated according to sex and had their material and spiritual needs provided for by a range of specialist staff attached to the institution.[42] Beyond the use of plague hospitals and home confinement, other forms of containment were adopted, such as general quarantines and *cordons sanitaire*. At Florence in 1630, women and children were ordered to remain at home, while at Rome in 1656 the Trastevere area was walled off (which may have been responsible for keeping mortality rates in Rome significantly lower than those of other towns).[43] In 1631, the entire Florentine state was placed under a general quarantine, though this was difficult to implement and soldiers were deployed to enforce plague regulations, a measure we also find in France.[44] *Cordons sanitaire* were also put in place between states, which may have played a role in preventing the spread of plague during the 1629–33 and 1656–7 outbreaks.[45]

Contact tracing was used as health authorities sought to find the person or persons responsible for starting an outbreak. Mass gatherings were clamped down on and commerce restricted. Men and women were employed to treat the sick and carry away the dead, while plague police were established to enforce regulations. The smaller size of the Italian city states meant that measures could

---

[40] For the text of the agreement, see: Cipolla, *Fighting the Plague*, pp. 111–15.
[41] Alfani and Murphy, 'Lethal Epidemics', 328; Tomić and Blažina, *Expelling the Plague*, pp. 106–7.
[42] Cipolla, *Cristofano and the Plague*, pp. 21–5; Crawshaw, 'Beasts of Burial'; Crawshaw, 'Invention of Quarantine'; Crawshaw, *Plague Hospitals*, p. 3; Henderson, *Florence Under Siege*, pp. 9, 183–5; Palmer, 'Control of Plague'.
[43] Cipolla, *Faith*, p. 69; Cipolla, *Fighting the Plague*, pp. 17–18; Henderson, 'Invisible Enemy', p. 31.
[44] Cipolla, *Faith*, p. 23.
[45] Alfani, 'Decline of Italy', p. 266; Henderson, *Florence Under Siege*, pp. 9, 26–7.

be implemented widely more easily than in large kingdoms such as France. In June 1631, the *Magistrato di Sanità* in Florence issued instructions to be applied in all five districts of the Florentine state. They appointed five commissioners-general, each of whom was a nobleman, with their orders stating that 'any spread and increase of that disease accrues for the most part from the people's disobedience and lack of observance of the proper ordinances which have been generally issued'. The commissioners were given 'supreme authority' to enforce these plague ordinances in their districts. They were to travel around their districts and learn the state of the disease, and, if the ordinances were not being followed, they were to take any action they deemed necessary to ensure that the measures were enforced. To pay for the anti-plague actions, they were first to seek contributions from the localities, but they were then to make up any shortfall from state funds.[46] Overall, the Italian methods formed the key responses to plague in early modern Europe and were used in various combinations and at different times in different places.

England

Italian plague measures were well known and admired by political elites in sixteenth-century England, where the first comprehensive measures were introduced in January 1518 by Henry VIII's chief minister, Cardinal Wolsey.[47] Although they were initially only concerned with London, these measures were steadily extended to other parts of the kingdom over the following decades.[48] If they were limited in comparison to those procedures then used in other parts of Europe, the London instructions included key aspects of anti-plague legislation which would remain in place until the disappearance of the disease, such as marking out infected houses. Like the monarchs of sixteenth-century France and Spain, the English Crown was particularly concerned about the health of its capital. Paul Slack argues it was the central state which devised the plague strategy in England, similar to the situation in northern Italy. Slack identifies three key stages in this process: first, Wolsey's 1518 regulations for London; second, the new set of plague regulations Elizabeth I's Privy Council issued in 1578; third, the anti-plague measures introduced under Charles I in the 1630s.[49] Slack also observes that the major innovations in plague control in England were not taken during major outbreaks as 'there was little opportunity to develop new policies', but that 'innovation occurred when relatively minor outbreaks of plague seemed to aggravate other pressing social problems,

---

[46] Cipolla, *Faith*, pp. 93, 95–6.   [47] Henderson, *Florence Under Siege*, pp. 3–4.

[48] Slack, *Impact*, pp. 201–2. For regulations coming from Henry VIII's fear of disease and implemented in the previous year, see: Roger, 'Quarantine Regulations'.

[49] For the latter, see especially: Slack, *Impact*, pp. 199–226.

especially in London'.[50] If England was similar to France in terms of wider societal problems, and particularly the growth of poverty, influencing public health regulations, it was quite different in terms of the involvement of central government in the management of plague, as these tended to occur in France during severe outbreaks.

While the comparatively late introduction of Italian-style anti-plague measures has often led England to be labelled backwards in terms of public health, Carole Rawcliffe has shown that late medieval English urban governments did have coherent strategies for combatting epidemic diseases, which were based around environmental issues, such as the cleaning of streets.[51] Recently, Charles Udale has shown that local authorities, on their own initiative and without pressure from the central state, were responsible for introducing key plague-control measures, particularly the pest houses which appeared in England from the 1530s.[52] The methods favoured by English towns, whereby household quarantine was the preferred method and pest houses were used for those who were unable to receive treatment at home, were similar to those favoured by their neighbours in northern France and the Low Countries. Certainly, the Crown provided little support to local authorities and measures were not always enforced. It was not until 1564, following complaints from the Privy Council about London's slackness in enforcing the confinement of the sick, that guards were sent to monitor houses and supplies provided to the enclosed. However, there was little in the way of taxation levied to support the anti-plague measures, which were inconsistent and varied from outbreak to outbreak. Nonetheless, by the 1570s, printed plague ordinances were circulated for various English towns and anti-plague measures adopted more widely than ever before.[53]

The war against plague in England was given a further impetus by the end of the decade, with the formulation of new ordinances in 1578. These were developed at the impetus of William Cecil, Elizabeth I's chief minister, and they were inspired by measures used on the continent, especially in Italy, and included input from Council of Physicians (which Wolsey had established in 1518). Observing that anti-plague regulations were not being enforced consistently, the Privy Council had the new regulations printed and attempted to have them implemented across the kingdom, employing the justices of the peace to oversee them at a parish level and report back to the Privy Council. This was a degree of state centralisation which would not be seen in France until several

---

[50] Slack, *Impact*, p. 200.
[51] Rawcliffe, *Urban Bodies*. For instance, Slack writes of England being a 'benighted, backward country' in terms of anti-plague measures in comparison to France or Italy: Slack, *Impact*, p. 201.
[52] Udale, 'Household Quarantine'; Udale, 'Pesthouses'; Newman, 'Bubonic Plague'.
[53] Slack, *Impact*, p. 205.

decades later, though many of the measures would be similar. The 1578 ordinances included a range of measures, from raising taxes to cover plague costs to regulations regarding the clothing and bedding of the sick. If the Privy Council had concerns about how far previous regulations had been enforced, recent work on English towns shows that the Elizabethan ordinances were being implemented.[54]

Further government intervention in plague measures came in 1630, when a mild bout of plague struck London. Whereas home isolation had been the favoured method of isolating the sick in England, the Privy Council pushed for the increased use of plague hospitals from the 1630s, with the Saint-Louis plague hospital, established at Paris in 1607, proposed as the model for London by the king's French physician, Sir Theodore de Mayerne, who had served as Henry IV's personal physician and had direct experience of the measures employed in France.[55] In some ways, this was an early example of the French style of plague care overtaking Italy in terms of influence, a process that would not take place more fully until the eighteenth century (although these measures were fundamentally those which had been devised in Italy in the first instance). While he was a Protestant, Mayerne was a strong advocate of the Bourbon model of plague care, the foundations of which were laid down by Henry IV. This model was based around the strict application of quarantine and the extensive use of plague hospitals, and Mayerne wanted to see it implemented in England. He also wanted overall plague control in London to be overseen by a permanent health board with extensive powers, staffed by representatives from the city council, the Privy Council and with the presence of two bishops. This was like the health boards used in France by the early seventeenth century, which had a similar composition although they were local rather than national and included regional royal officials rather than members of the king's council. Certainly, it was getting closer to the pluralistic plague model used in France, which was dependent on different officials and institutions working together. In any case, this was to remain theoretical as these measures were not implemented, nor was there a monumental royal plague hospital constructed in London along the lines of Paris. These issues arose again during the major plague of 1665, when the ongoing preference for home isolation was strongly criticised on the basis that it needlessly infected the healthy. To avoid this, the sick should be removed to a plague hospital where they would receive medical care. These ideas underpinned the 1666 'Rules and Orders', devised by the Privy Council, which remodelled the 1578 plague regulations and insisted

---

[54] Udale, 'Household Quarantine'.
[55] For the 1594 London pesthouse, see: Columbus, 'Plague Pesthouses'.

on the importance of bringing the infected to plague hospitals, while the healthy who had been in contact with them were to quarantine at home.[56] Yet the 1665 plague was the last time the disease visited England and these measures were not employed.

The Low Countries

Towns in the Low Countries began to develop anti-plague legislation from the mid-fifteenth century. As with other parts of Europe, existing sanitary measures informed the regulations, which also sought to separate the sick from the healthy. Like England, historians have tended to take a dismissive view of late medieval anti-plague measures in the Low Countries, which are unfavourably compared with those in Italy.[57] Yet recent work by Janna Coomans and others has shown that there was a strong tradition of municipal involvement in public health long before the central state became involved in the seventeenth century.[58] In Utrecht, the city council collated its measures in a 1474 plague ordinance which was employed during plague outbreaks for the next two centuries. The measures devised in the towns of the Netherlands during the fifteenth century were focused on keeping the infected separate from the healthy, typically by having them confined to their homes and carrying a white stick if they left so that people could avoid them. Infected houses were marked out with a bundle of straw.[59] As has been noted, this was similar to the situation in northern France and England.

By the sixteenth century, most major towns across the Low Countries had comprehensive plague ordinances, which were generally similar in character.[60] As in France, towns shared anti-plague measures and knowledge adopted from elsewhere as needed. The regulations were broadly like those issued in other parts of Europe and focused on controlling the movement of people, animals and goods, as well as creating a salubrious environment through the cleaning of streets and removal of waste. Urban governments were also concerned about the flight of citizens and issued threats of punishment, such as loss of citizenship, to any who did not return. These sanctions may have been effective as mass desertions became unusual during the sixteenth century in the Low Countries, which is in contrast to France where they remained common – despite similar threats – through to the plague of Provence in 1720. Food regulations formed a key part of the anti-plague legislation, especially regarding access to markets and the quality of goods, concerns common to governments across Europe as substandard food was thought to be a key source of infection, a belief which also

---

[56] *Rules and orders* (1666).

[57] Noordegraaf and Valk, *De gave Gods*; Kerkhoff, *Per imperatief plakkaat*.

[58] Coomans, *Urban Health*, esp. chapter 5.   [59] Rommes, 'Dutch Experience', p. 56.

[60] For what comes below, see: Coomans, *Urban Health*, pp. 216–51.

helped inform the conceptual links between poverty and plague. Neither health boards nor plague hospitals were common in the Low Countries before the late sixteenth century. Urban governments preferred to use the existing medical infrastructure and hospitals, often setting aside designated areas of hospitals for the use of plague-infected patients, which we also find in northern France with the *hôtels Dieu* (general hospitals). Doctors and other medical officials were already employed by urban governments in the Low Countries for a variety of tasks, for which plague care became one. However, the input of medical professionals into urban plague policy is uncertain, in contrast to what was found in other parts of Europe.

In terms of the involvement of central government, the *Staten Generaal*, established in 1588, did not start intervening in plague measures until the 1660s, which Kerkhoff argues was the reason why plague outbreaks stopped striking the Low Countries after this decade.[61] Kerkhoff shows that Gaspar Fagel, then pensionary (legal representative) to Haarlem's town council, advocated stricter quarantine measures after looking at the measures used in neighbouring states, including the Southern Netherlands which were under Spanish rule. Interestingly, Habsburg rulers in the Netherlands may have had a longer history of involvement in plague care. At Douai, in the sixteenth century Philip II granted the town council the right to use revenues gathered on taxes to pay for the support of the infected poor.[62] During the same period, Cambrai made copies of quarantine regulations Emperor Wenceslaus IV of Luxembourg had made for the city in 1388 and 1395, probably as a means to strengthen their authority to issue such instructions in the sixteenth century.[63] We find state powers in the Southern Netherlands helping towns implement plague measures. In 1667 – at the same time as the Bourbon monarchy was supporting its towns in the north to cope with the plague – the Habsburg *conseil privé* at Brussels ordered the Estates of Cambrai to pay for the costs of treating plague victims in the city, while the following year it issued instructions ordering the nobles and clergy to observe the measures which the city council had ordered against plague.[64] We can also find Habsburg rulers supporting urban governments to manage plague outbreaks when we turn our attention to Spain.

Spain

The initial impetus for the development of plague-management schemes in Spain came from the towns, which as in both England and the Low Countries preferred a looser application of quarantine measures. Kristy Wilson Bowers

---

[61] Kerkhoff, *Per imperatief plakkaat*, p. 271.   [62] AM Douai CC 721.
[63] AM Cambrai AA 26.   [64] AM Cambrai BB 2, fol. 333v.

has shown that Seville implemented a plague system which sought to balance the need to protect the city against the disease with desirability of allowing commerce to continue.[65] This system was designed to slow down the pace at which plague spread without completely shutting down the city.[66] As in France, the introduction of plague-relief systems provided a more compassionate way to treat the sick. While Santander initially ordered the expulsion of the plague sick in 1596, this measure was overturned and the infected were instead hospitalised and provided with care. Municipal plague taxes became common in Spain, as they were in France, such as that levied at Bilbao in 1598, which helped pay for the increased plague infrastructure.[67]

In the sixteenth century, the kings of Spain focused on maintaining watch over outbreaks at Madrid, but they made little effort to impose public health measures on other civic governments. Managing epidemics was the concern of local authorities and the Crown only stepped in when asked to do so. Spanish kings started to take more direct involvement in the management of plague outbreaks from the second half of the sixteenth century. Philip II's micromanagement of his empire and desire for information extended to plague outbreaks. He corresponded more extensively than any of his predecessors with local authorities during plague outbreaks and took an interest in medicine, which increased the knowledge of plague care at court. Philip II offered advice to urban governments, who increasingly looked to the Crown to intervene in matters such as the lifting of quarantines. It was not that the Crown was enforcing measures, but that towns were seeking to co-opt its support (which we will also see for France). At this stage, the Crown's input was advisory and did not result in royal decrees. Nonetheless, Philip II's reign represented a key moment in royal interest in plague.

Philip tended to support the efforts of municipal councils. When complaints were made by the count of Villar against the town council of Seville's handling of the plague in the 1580s (particularly that they had not adequately kept the sick away from the healthy), the councillors wrote to the king to refute the allegations – and the king supported their actions.[68] The development of massive public health measures against plague, especially the building, staffing and supply of plague hospitals, crippled urban budgets and led to petitions to the king for financial support. For instance, by mid-July 1581, when plague was declining, Seville had spent 17,416,000 *maravedis* (46,433 ducats) on plague, of which 13,676,000 *maravedis* (36,469 ducats) had been paid for from money raised by loans and the rest was still owed.[69] To help cover the costs of plague

---

[65] Bowers, *Plague and Public Health*.   [66] Bowers, *Plague and Public Health*, pp. 56–7.
[67] Bennassar, *Grandes épidémies*, p. 54.
[68] Bowers, *Plague and Public Health*, pp. 26, 89–90; Cook and Cook, *Plague Files*, pp. 105–8.
[69] Cook and Cook, *Plague Files*, p. 109

relief, the Spanish Crown granted towns the right to use revenue generated from the excise tax known as the *sisa*.[70] The Crown helped in other ways too, particularly in supporting the town council in requisitioning buildings for use as hospitals or convalescence centres, or helping to organise food supplies by allowing quarantine regulations to be sidestepped.[71] Madrid saw the highest levels of involvement from the Crown and it was unusual amongst Spanish towns in the levels of royal involvement it had in anti-plague measures. Yet this could also benefit Madrid, as the municipal council could petition the Crown to use its authority and resources to support their efforts. For example, they had the Crown and royal council of Castile use their authority to compel doctors and surgeons to treat the city's infected.[72]

It was the 'Atlantic Plague' of 1596–1602 which really led the Crown to take an interest in plague management and seek to coordinate efforts against the disease. Cities remained the key agents, though the Crown increased its correspondence with urban elites and asked for regular sanitary reports. As in France, the Spanish monarchs were particularly concerned about the types of treatments which were being given to plague victims. In 1599, Philip III had his chief physician, Luis Mercado, publish his plague tract, first in Latin and then in Castilian, at royal expense so that people would 'understand and know with certainty which disease it is and how they should protect themselves'.[73] It was during this plague that the *corregidores* (the leading royal official in the localities) really began to take a role in plague management, instigating quarantine instructions to the towns in their jurisdictions as well as organising the distribution of medicines and the supply of other goods.[74] In this respect, their role was often supportive and they promoted urban interests with the king, though they could also impose measures directly as required.[75]

Rumours of conspiracies to deliberately spread plague during the outbreak of the 1630s led the Crown to take more interventionist measures, such as stopping persons arriving from France, though it was not really until the 1670s that the key developments took place in centralising the management of plague. The Spanish Crown first collected information about outbreaks of plague and then issued a standard set of regulations to be employed against the disease. As in France, the Crown did little to innovate in terms of the methods used against plague, which remained based around the control of people and goods. The difference was that the Crown now gathered information and distributed standardised instructions across Spain. Yet urban authorities remained in control of the actual implementation of these measures. During the plague of Provence,

---

[70] Cook and Cook, *Plague Files*, p. 86   [71] Cook and Cook, *Plague Files*, pp. 78, 82, 89.
[72] MacKay, *Castilian Plague*, p. 29.   [73] MacKay, *Castilian Plague*, p. 226.
[74] MacKay, *Castilian Plague*, pp. 65–6.   [75] Bennassar, *Grandes épidémies*, pp. 27–31.

Philip V (also a Bourbon monarch) created the *Junta Suprema de Sanidad* which oversaw the prevention of epidemics throughout the entire Iberian Peninsula.[76] It remained in operation after the plague of Provence had ended and sought to prevent plague from entering Spain, especially from North Africa, and it oversaw the response to other infectious diseases, such as yellow fever, until it was dissolved in 1857.[77]

***

This brief sketch has sought to outline the broader context in which developments in France occurred. We saw how towns in England, the Low Countries and northern France preferred a system of plague management based around home isolation, although the monarchies of these kingdoms preferred the stricter application of Italian-style quarantine methods. The interplay between local and central authorities was complex, especially in geographically large states where it was more difficult for central authorities to impose regulations across a wide area. If central control of plague management in England and Italy came early, this was less so in the Low Countries and Spain, where plague measures were overwhelmingly local initiatives developed by municipalities, with central state intervention coming later – a process we shall examine now as we look at France.

3 Towns and the Development of Plague-Control Systems in France

This section shows that plague-control regulations in France were an urban innovation. Long before the monarchy became involved in the organisation of public health efforts, urban governments worked together to share information and coordinate their efforts, particularly seeking to prevent communication between infected and healthy areas. While, as we shall see in the next section, a range of other institutions contributed to the fight against plague, municipal governments remained central to the implementation of these measures right through to the eighteenth century. We can trace the origins of these measures to the fifteenth century, especially in towns of the Midi. As public health measures became increasingly comprehensive from the devastating plagues of the later sixteenth century, municipal resources were stretched to breaking point and they sought assistance from the monarch and his provincial agents. While historians have tended to minimise the impact of plague on the countryside, this section shows that it decimated rural areas. Urban governments monitored surrounding villages and worked with rural communities to treat outbreaks and prevent the

---

[76] Bowers, *Plague and Public Health*, pp. 90–1.   [77] Peris, 'Junta Suprema de Sanidad'.

infection from spreading into towns. Overall, urban governments spearheaded the development of a sophisticated public health system, the key elements of which would persist in France for centuries.

The Emergence of Plague Regulations

From the late fifteenth century, urban governments across France formulated ordinances to be observed during times of plague.[78] Urban communities in the southeast of the kingdom developed the first plague-control measures derived from ideas about contagion, while those in the north and west continued to focus on sanitary legislation for longer. This was probably because these towns were adopting measures used by their neighbours in northern Italy, whereas northern towns kept broadly in line with the practices used by their neighbours in the Low Countries. Amiens' municipal council stated that their adoption of cleaning regimes during times of plague derived from knowledge of developments in Lille, Saint-Omer, Tournai and Valenciennes.[79] Rather than place the infected and suspected in quarantine, many northern towns simply burned down infected houses and drove the inhabitants out to live or die in the surrounding fields.[80] Gradually the use of quarantine and plague hospitals spread throughout the north during the sixteenth century, which reduced the severity of these measures.

Regional differences became less pronounced over time and by the late sixteenth century most French towns were issuing the same general provisions, which were based around three key principles: (1) controlling the movement of people, animals and goods; (2) providing specialised medical care, especially to the poor; (3) creating a salubrious environment. By isolating the sick, cleansing their goods and imposing sanitary regulations, they took practical steps to limit the spread and severity of outbreaks. Copies of plague ordinances were kept in city archives and reissued when required.[81] They were announced throughout the streets and pinned to the customary locations; with the expansion of printing, they were distributed widely. Although some modifications were made to the rules over times (for instance, the introduction of health passports during the sixteenth century allowed greater freedom of movement), the same standard provisions existed right through to the eighteenth century.[82] Anyone who broke

---

[78] For examples of plague ordinances, see: AM Lyon 3GG 006; AM Aix-en-Provence AA 14, fols. 621–8, BB 100, fols. 75–95v; BNF Moreau 806, fols. 97–101; Garnier (ed.), *Journal de Gabriel Breunot*, vol. III, pp. 91–6; Magen, 'Registres consulaires'.

[79] AM Amiens BB 9, fol. 124.

[80] Boutiot, *Pestes de Troyes*, p. 6; Guilbert, 'Châlons-sur-Marne', p. 1293.

[81] See, for instance, at Lyon: AM Lyon 3GG 013–24.

[82] AM Lyon 3GG 014. Grenoble was already issuing health passports by 1521: AM Grenoble BB 6, fol. 48v. For health passports, see: Bamji, 'Health Passes'.

the plague regulations faced punishment. When merchants from Grenoble complained about the prohibition on attending the Lyon fairs in 1521, the town council threatened to banish anyone who infringed the travel regulations along with their families.[83] Plague prisons were established, such as that made in the belfry at Troyes in 1518, while those who committed the most serious punishments were to be shot.[84] In 1597 gallows were erected on the main bridge leading into Dijon, where those who broke the plague regulations were to be shot and have their bodies displayed.[85]

The development of plague ordinances reflected a growing acceptance of contagion theory amongst the urban elites of France, which probably resulted from both a century's worth of observation about how the disease hit towns and the increased spread of medical knowledge about plague. As we saw in the Introduction, there was an overlap between ideas about contagion and older understandings about the role of corrupt air in spreading disease. In 1623, Laon's municipal council implemented measures both to prevent contact with the infected and 'to avoid infection from bad air', while Dijon's ordinances contained rules informed by ideas about contagion and out of a concern to avoid 'bad air'.[86] The regulations also reflected growing belief in 'contingent contagion', particularly that the poor were especially susceptible to infection. The plague ordinance issued at Amiens in July 1514 was almost entirely concerned with regulating and restricting the circulation of foreign vagrants in the town. Debates in both the *parlement* of Paris and civic council chambers saw them as two sides of the same coin, while Dijon's regulations were 'prepared both because of the disease of plague and for the poor'.[87]

The development of plague regulations and the creation of specialist hospitals and health boards resulted in the need to hire people to treat the sick, transport the infected and enforce regulations. While these positions were well paid, they could be unpopular due to the dangers involved. Urban governments enlisted the support of other agencies to help with recruitment difficulties. When physicians proved slow to offer their services to Rouen's municipal council during the plague outbreak of 1538, the town council obtained an order from the *parlement* instructing the college of physicians in the city

---

[83] AM Grenoble BB 6, fol. 82. This was a toughening of the stance in 1497 when merchants who had broken the plague rules and attended the Lyon fairs were quarantined in Grenoble upon their return: AM Grenoble BB 2, fol. 187.

[84] Boutiot, *Pestes de Troyes*, p. 21 ; Magen, 'Registres consulaires', p. 109 ; Canard, *Pestes*, p. 147.

[85] Garnier (ed.), *Journal de Gabriel Breunot*, vol. III, p. 95.

[86] Matton, *Inventaire sommaire, Laon*, p. 97 ; Garnier (ed.), *Journal de Gabriel Breunot*, vol. III, p. 96.

[87] Tuetey (ed.), *Registres des délibérations, Paris, 1527–1539*, pp. 168–9 ; Garnier (ed.), *Journal de Gabriel Breunot*, vol. III, pp. 91–6.

immediately to elect one of their number to tend the sick, with the threat of punishment should they refuse.[88] It was important to have medical experts ready not just to treat the sick but to identify the presence of plague. A precise definition was crucial, as the preventative measures adopted in response to plague were more extensive and onerous than those employed against other infectious diseases. When an outbreak of suspected plague struck Rouen in December 1537, the town council held three separate meetings to discuss the question of diagnosis. The meetings were attended by two physicians in civic employment and a further three hired to provide additional opinions on the aetiology of the disease. When all five agreed that plague was indeed present in the town, the municipal council immediately set in train the mechanisms customarily taken to manage outbreaks of the disease.[89]

French municipal councils often preferred to remain in direct control of the implementation of plague measures into the sixteenth century, in contrast to Italy where specialist health boards were common from the fifteenth century. As with the development of measures based around contagion, the formation of separate health boards was first adopted in towns lying close to Italy, with Bourg-en-Bresse – the first town to use a plague hospital – establishing a health board in 1504, though many towns did not establish health boards until instructed to do so by royal order in the seventeenth century.[90] French health boards tended to be temporary even in the seventeenth century, which reflects the ongoing local nature of plague management. In contrast to the central state institutions established in Venice or Milan, most French towns could not afford to maintain a permanent health board, nor did most see any need to do so. Nonetheless, they could be summoned at the first sign of plague. In 1628, following the recording of a single death from plague at Agen, the health board immediately convened and met twice a week even though more deaths were not immediately forthcoming.[91] They also possessed extensive powers. The health board established at Narbonne in December 1591 was composed of twelve men who were under the authority of the town council but who had full powers to act on all measures relating to plague.[92] Where the earliest health boards were dominated by municipal councils, with the growth in polycentric plague care from the later sixteenth century, health boards came to be composed of multiple authorities. In the 1580s, the health board at Troyes (established in 1562) was reconfigured to consist of the municipal council, clergy and

---

[88] AD Seine-Maritime 3E 1 Rouen AA 14, fol. 41. See also for Paris: Tuetey (ed.), *Registres, Paris, 1527–1539*, p. 169.

[89] AD Seine-Maritime 3ᴱ 1 Rouen A 14, fol. 48.   [90] Guiart, *Histoire de la peste*, p. 15.

[91] Magen, 'Registres consulaires', p. 123.

[92] AM Narbonne BB 5, fol. 408–409v. See also: BB 5, fol. 412v.

representatives of each quarter of the city, with a royal officer presiding over it.[93] In September 1721, the *indendant* of Moulins ordered each town in his jurisdiction to establish a health board composed of both the town council and the clergy, which was to assemble each week to discuss measures to prevent the plague in Provence spreading.[94]

Plague Police

Long before Louis XV's soldiers entered Marseille in 1720, municipal governments appointed their own armed police forces to enforce plague regulations and maintain order. The development of anti-plague measures based on ideas about contagion from the later fifteenth century amongst urban governments made it important to control the movement of people and goods. Rather than establish a health board, many French towns initially nominated a *capitaine de santé* to oversee the implementation of the plague regulations. When plague struck Toulouse in 1516, the *capitouls* appointed a *capitaine de santé* (designated as an 'officer of the town hall') who was given an armed guard 'to execute the functions of his office, of which the principal [one] is to contain the plague sick and prevent them from leaving'.[95] Grenoble's *capitaine de santé* held considerable powers and responsibilities including: managing the plague staff, especially the guard; orchestrating the monitoring of the gates; organising street cleaning; signing health certificates and determining the length of quarantines.[96] In effect, he was undertaking all the duties of a health board. At Grenoble, the first captains were physicians, though they soon became non-medical and included the former *consul*, Guillaume Lérisse, who nonetheless composed a popular plague treatise based on his experiences during the severe plague of the 1590s.[97]

To enforce the plague regulations and maintain them, the *capitaines de santé*, or those responsible for overseeing the town's plague response, were provided with a police force which was often initially drawn from existing municipal officers (in the early sixteenth century, for instance, Dijon's *échevins* tasked their municipal sergeants with acting as the plague police).[98] Yet the number of men that town councils appointed to the role was typically small. Despite being one of the largest cities of the kingdom, Lyon had thirteen men to enforce the plague ordinances.[99] To help offset the low numbers, urban governments

---

[93] Boutiot, *Pestes de Troyes*, pp. 37–8.   [94] Parmentier, *Archives de Nevers*, vol. I, p. 215

[95] Roucaud, *Peste à Toulouse*, p. 48.   [96] Chavant, *Peste à Grenoble*, pp. 53–4.

[97] Lérisse, *Petit traité de la peste*.

[98] Gouvenain, *Inventaire sommaire, Dijon*, vol. 1, p. 50. For Italian plague police, see: Assereto, 'Polizia sanitaria'.

[99] Canard, *Pestes*, p. 147.

utilised the obligation of *guet* (which obliged heads of household to provide guard duty) to support the plague police in monitoring entry to the town. Yet recruitment remained a problem because the wealthier classes – who formed the backbone of city militias – frequently fled during plague outbreaks. At Troyes, the guard was divided into the *hommes de fer* (merchants, townspeople and heads of household) and the *hommes de pourpoint* (workers and artisans), with the *hommes de fer* being summoned for the guard during times of plague.[100] In 1564, Lyon's rulers informed Charles IX that so many townspeople had fled that there were not enough people of a suitable social standing left to guard the city.[101] The same was as true for small towns as it was for large cities. At Mauriac in 1505, 'the inhabitants of the town left and went to forests, villages and *affars* [a type of rural holding] to make small huts [so that] only four or five people [presumably those of a suitable social standing] remained in Mauriac to guard the property of the town'.[102] In an early manifestation of the use of soldiers to help town councils enforce plague regulations, Amiens hired mercenaries during the plague outbreaks of 1493 and 1519 to guard the city gates against incomers and to prevent townspeople from leaving, while at Nevers in 1518 sergeants of the count of Nevers helped enforced the town council's plague regulations.[103]

It could be difficult to compel even those who remained to undertake guard duty. In October 1588, Auriol's town council observed that the gates were poorly guarded because men refused to undertake this service.[104] In 1665, they levied fines on any person who refused to go on guard during times of plague.[105] Other councils tried to find a solution which both allowed people to leave and secured the town. At Mirecourt in the Vosges region of eastern France in 1632, the council forbade any townspeople from fleeing without having (1) left a replacement to perform their guard duty and (2) paying three months of plague taxes. The guards on Mirecourt's gates were instructed not to let anyone leave without the mayor's written authorisation.[106] At Narbonne, any householder who fled had to leave paid guards to guard their property.[107] Preventing criminality – especially robbery – was a key concern for municipal governments, as plague outbreaks provided ideal conditions for criminals because the flight of the wealthy left numerous houses empty. At Angoulême in 1502, the town council sought to 'quickly establish order and police as the few people who reside there are oppressed and outraged by a large number of bad boys who

---

[100] Boutiot, *Pestes de Troyes*, p. 9.   [101] Canard, *Pestes*, p. 18.
[102] Boudet and Grand, *Documents inédits*, p. 62.
[103] AM Amiens BB 16, fol. 265, BB 22, fol. 13 ; Boutillier, *Inventaire sommaire, Nevers*, p. 47.
[104] AC Auriol BB 4, fol. 378.   [105] AC Auriol BB 9, fol. 70v.
[106] Bouchot, 'Peste de Lorraine', p. 147.   [107] AM Narbonne BB 5, fol. 421.

assemble at night and make many evils and insults', for which purpose they hired a captain and appointed a guard.[108] In 1516, Nevers paid the *prévôt* and fourteen guards to police the town day and night during the plague, as the wealthier inhabitants had fled and their houses 'were in danger of being robbed and looted by many bad boys who came there daily to cause harm'.[109] Certainly, towns became a magnet for criminals drawn by the prospect of empty houses to rob. During the plague which hit Laon two years later, the town council paid guards to prevent the 'bad boys who come at night to loot and rob the houses of the townspeople'.[110] An examination of royal letters of remission supports the impression of widespread criminality given in the municipal deliberations during plague outbreaks. In 1566, Charles IX granted a letter of remission to Jean Rion who during the 'great contagion of plague' was appointed to pursue the 'thieves and night runners (*courreurs de nuit*)' who pillaged abandoned houses in Ennezat in Auvergne (and who had been charged with murder).[111] On the other hand, Louis XII pardoned one Jean Guillaume from Langres for thefts he had committed when the plague ravaged the town in 1499.[112]

Towns employed deterrents to prevent criminality in the first place. During the plague outbreak at Albi in 1521, thieves, plague spreaders, highway robbers and 'rebels' (*croquants* and *ribauds*) were hanged, drawn and quartered as an example to others.[113] During the same outbreak, the municipal deliberations of Angoulême note that the region was invested with '*laquais et bandoliers*' [armed men and their hangers-on] who were 'in great number in the fields' [i.e. the countryside] and causing many 'evils, [and keeping] in fear the towns of Poitiers, Niort and Tours'.[114] The link between criminality and sedition during plague became stronger during the plagues of the seventeenth century, which occurred against a backdrop of widespread social discontent that led to a series of popular rebellions in the 1630s and 1640s.[115] Existing social tensions were exacerbated during plague times, when resources were stretched and a sharp distinction drawn between the wealthy urban classes who fled the towns and the poor who remained. At Clermont-Ferrand in 1631, rumours that the wealthier were secretly taking grain supplies with them led to municipal fears that the poor would go into revolt.[116] At the first appearance of plague in Rodez in 1652, the council noted that the wealthier were fleeing and bringing grain supplies with them, which caused food shortages in the town.[117] During the same outbreak, Agen's health board feared that a lack of food in the city was about

---

[108] Lièvre, *Épidémies à Angoulême*, p. 10.   [109] Boutillier, *Inventaire sommaire, Nevers*, p. 45.
[110] Matton, *Inventaire sommaire, Laon*, p. 13.   [111] AN JJ//264.   [112] AN JJ/226/A-JJ//235
[113] AD Tarn, 4 EDT AA 4, fol. 78.   [114] Lièvre, *Épidémies à Angoulême*, pp. 17–18.
[115] Mousnier, *Fureurs paysannes* ; Porchev, *Soulèvements populaires* ; Bercé, *Croquants et nu-pieds*.
[116] Lucenet, *Grandes pestes*, p. 140.   [117] Affre, *Inventaire sommaire, Rodez*, p. 11.

to push the lower classes into revolt.[118] Plague and famine at Angoulême in the early 1630s was followed by a mass popular revolt in the region in 1636.[119] Beyond food shortages, opposition towards the enforcement of strict anti-plague measures may have contributed towards instances of popular discontent. Even Louis XV's physicians, François Chicoyneau, who led the initial – and incorrect – royal investigation into plague at Marseille in 1720 and who observed the use of soldiers to impose a cordon sanitaire in Provence, and his successor to the post, Jean-Baptiste Sénac, wrote against the 'violence done to freedom' and the 'insults performed on people's rights' by the forcible impos-ition of quarantine measures.[120] Yet the use of punitive force, or the threat of using it, had long been employed in France to enforce disease-control measures. Concerns with sedition during the plague outbreak of the 1630s increased the Bourbon monarchy's concern to manage plague outbreaks and led to plans to despatch soldiers to towns to enforce order, as a lack of municipal manpower made it difficult for urban governments to prevent criminality. The most common crime during the outbreak at Marseille in the 1720s remained the burglary of abandoned buildings, with the city's physician, Jean-Baptiste Bertrand, observing that when plague had struck the city in 1580 and 1630 there had also been widespread disorder.[121] It was intervention of the army that brought an end to widespread criminality at Marseille; yet, as we shall see in the following section, the use of soldiers to enforce law and order during plague outbreaks was not a development of the eighteenth century.

Paying for Plague Care

The introduction of plague ordinances created a major new source of expend-iture for urban governments, particularly because of the costs of constructing and maintaining plague hospitals and quarantine centres, where the sick were tended by medical professionals and provided with food and medicine. These costs, modest at first, rocketed from the later sixteenth century. As well as the extended severity and duration of plague outbreaks, there was a massive growth in poverty. Given that anti-plague systems were largely based around providing free care and medical treatment to the poor, the costs quickly spiralled. While we can find some instances of wealthier members of society being admitted to plague hospitals, these institutions unquestionably became overwhelmingly associated with the treatment of the poor. The entrance records for the plague hospital for Tours in 1584 show that it was without exception the poor who were

---

[118] Magen, 'Registres consulaires', p. 136.   [119] Lièvre, *Épidémies à Angoulême*, pp. 80–5.
[120] Cited in: Jones, 'Plague and its Metaphors', pp. 115–16.
[121] Takeda, *Crown and Commerce*, pp. 111, 144.

admitted.[122] Both in France and across Europe more widely, social elites increasingly saw plague as principally a disease of the poor.[123] Arising during the fifteenth century, this identification between plague and poverty, as Samuel Cohn and John Henderson have shown, became stronger during the course of the sixteenth century and remained strong into the eighteenth century.[124] When plague ravaged Marseille in 1721, for instance, Avignon's *consuls* decided to enclose the city's homeless poor.[125] Urban councils drew a distinction between the 'deserving' local poor, who were to be supported during plague times, and 'undeserving' foreign vagrants, who were to be expelled. Town councils decided how the deserving poor were to be provided with the resources they required. Their principal concern was in giving to local poor rather than outsiders, who were seen as an undeserving drain on resources. During the plague outbreak at Narbonne in the early 1630s, the town council installed a committee to work with the clergy and decide parish by parish who were permitted to remain (native poor) and who were to be expelled (foreign poor).[126]

The belief that the poor were the principal carriers of plague developed alongside the growth of civic humanism, a movement which emphasised that urban rulers had a duty to treat those who could not afford specialist medical care. In the early days of the development of anti-plague systems, urban governments drew on longstanding conceptions of charity to help bolster municipal expenditure by raising funds through donation. In 1459, Rodez drew up a list of contributors who had helped meet the costs incurred by implementing the new plague regulations, while Grenoble's first plague hospital was established in 1485 as the result of a testamentary bequest.[127] Charity remained an important source of income well into the sixteenth century. When Narbonne's *consuls* decided to construct a plague hospital in 1565, they appointed a commission specifically to make 'the search [for gifts] to complete the hospital', while Lyon expanded its St Laurent plague hospital in the 1530s following a donation from a wealthy merchant.[128] In 1632, Troyes asked the town's wealthy women ('de la plus apparente condition') to go round

---

[122] AM Tours GG 2.

[123] For plague and poverty, see: Carmichael, *Plague and the Poor*; Cohn, *Cultures of Plague*, pp. 208–37; Crawshaw, *Plague Hospitals*, pp. 79–108; Henderson, *Florence Under Siege*, pp. 51–117; Murphy, 'Plague Hospitals'; Murphy, 'Poor Relief'; Pullan, 'Perceptions of the Poor', in Ranger and Slack, *Epidemics and Ideas*.

[124] Cohn, *Cultures of Plague*, pp. 210–13; Henderson, 'Charity and Welfare', p. 78.

[125] AD Vaucluse FRAD084_E Dépôt Avignon BB 93, fol. 95. On the association between poverty and disease in the eighteenth century, see: Siena, *Rotten Bodies*.

[126] AM Narbonne BB 18, fol. 153.

[127] Affre, *Inventaire sommaire, Rodez*, p. 54 ; Chavant, *Peste à Grenoble*, p. 6.

[128] AM Narbonne BB 2, fol. 17v; AM Lyon BB 55, fol. 106v, BB 67, fol. 8v.

each parish seeking donations to support the infected poor.[129] Plague care thus provided a further outlet for the wealthy to display charity.

Although charity remained an important source of income throughout the early modern period, donations were sporadic and town councils needed alternative sources of funding. While plague hospitals began as modest institutions in the late fifteenth century, those constructed to cope with the plagues of the late sixteenth and seventeenth centuries were extensive and housed large numbers of people. When Beauvais established a plague hospital in the 1620s, it placed an initial levy of 3,600 *livres* on the inhabitants, which was then followed by further levies of 3,000 *livres* and 4,000 *livres* as the costs rocketed. While the town's clergy also contributed 3,300 *livres*, even these sums were not enough and the town had to borrow a further 3,000 *livres*.[130] During the plague outbreak at Bordeaux in the 1640s, the town council were paying out up to 5,000 *livres* a month on the expenses of the city's two plague hospitals.[131] Such sums were far in excess of what municipal councils could hope to raise through charity alone, especially when outbreaks persisted for years, which we see when we look at Douai's finances during the plague of 1667–70 (see Table 1).

In both 1668–9 and 1669–70, Douai's costs exceeded municipal income. To avoid bankruptcy, the town council asked for advances on various payments, including that due for the town's fortifications. Nonetheless, even with this additional income, spending remained more than revenue.[132] It could take towns years to recover from the financial impact of a major outbreak of plague. In the 1720s, Marseille incurred debts of 1,472,894 *livres* due to the costs of combating plague – a statistic which highlights the scale of the burdens borne by municipal governments even during an outbreak which saw the greater use of central state resources than ever before.[133]

Table 1 Douai's finances during the plague of 1667–70.

Year	Total municipal expenditure (in *livres*)	Plague expenditure (in *livres*)	Plague expenditure as a percentage of total municipal expenditure
1667–8	6,698	4,233	63%
1668–9	42,612	36,677	86%
1669–70	14,327	10,323	72%

[129] Boutiot, *Pestes de Troyes*, p. 42.   [130] Rose, *Inventaire sommaire, Beauvais*, p. 30.
[131] Boisville, *Registres de la Jurade, Bordeaux*, vol. I, pp. 578, 580.
[132] AM Douai CC 1205, 1206, 1208, 1209.
[133] Carrière et al, *Marseille*, pp. 273, 333–4 ; Slack, 'Perceptions of Plague', pp. 144–5.

Urban governments took out loans to try and meet these increased costs. By 1564, Auch's *consuls* were already borrowing money to pay for medical staff, treatments and poor relief.[134] Loans became a standard way of meeting plague expenditure. In 1628, as soon as Auch's *consuls* heard of the presence of plague at Toulouse, they took out loans to hire medical staff and purchase medicines in case the disease struck the town.[135] They could perhaps hope that this would be a sound financial investment because if they were ready to act as soon as the first cases were discovered they could hope to prevent the high costs of a major outbreak. By 1631, as the plague entered its third year at Narbonne, the *consuls* took out multiple loans coming to thousands of *livres* to cover the costs of treating the poor.[136] When plague returned to Narbonne again in 1652, by the end of the year the *consuls* had mounted up loans totalling 21,000 *livres* to cover plague expenditure.[137] Despite taking extensive and early action to prevent plague taking hold in Bordeaux in 1629, the city suffered a major outbreak which persisted for several years. While it was one of the largest and richest cities in the kingdom, Bordeaux was soon financially exhausted and the heavily indebted city council was unable to pay its plague costs, so much so that in October 1630 the baker who supplied the plague hospital refused to provide any more bread, stating that he was already owed thousands of *livres*.[138] Urban governments faced lawsuits from their creditors. During the plague of the 1630s at Nice, men who had provided medicines and food to the town council took out legal cases against the *consuls* for failure of payment.[139] By 1632, the financially exhausted town had to renegotiate their contract with the physician Louis XIII had sent them and they resorted to taking out further loans to cover this and other plague costs.[140]

Town councils also placed levies on urban populations to pay for plague-relief schemes. When a severe outbreak of plague struck Saint-Flour in 1564 (which led to an expansion in the town's infrastructure to deal with plague and thus a rise in associated costs), the *consuls* revived a poor tax which had been established in the thirteenth century but which had fallen out of use during the Hundred Years' War.[141] Troyes used the *aumône générale* (a municipal tax for poor relief), which it tripled in 1632 to raise money to treat the poor in the plague hospital.[142] Yet raising money via existing taxes could be difficult to achieve during plague outbreaks. First, it was difficult to collect taxes from

[134] AD Gers 1Edépôt Auch BB 5, fol. 183v.   [135] AD Gers 1Edépôt Auch BB 6, fol. 272.

[136] AM Narbonne BB 18, fols. 62v, 67v, 173v.

[137] AM Narbonne BB 23, fols. 227, 240, 242v, 243v, 246v, 253v.

[138] Boisville, *Registres de la Jurade, Bordeaux*, vol. I, p. 548.

[139] AM Nice GG 70/4, GG 70/13.   [140] AM Nice GG 70/5, 70/14.

[141] Boudet and Grand, *Documents inédits*, pp. 75–6.

[142] Boutiot, *Pestes de Troyes*, p. 42. For the *aumône générale*, see : Fosseyeux, 'Taxe au pauvres'.

people who had fled, who also tended to be the wealthy. Second, townspeople could refuse to pay these taxes. In 1553, Beaune's *échevins* took out legal cases against the many inhabitants who refused to pay the plague tax. The lack of revenue raised through taxation forced the town council to take out loans, for which they used silver images of saints Peter and Paul as collateral.[143]

Difficulties in levying taxes led urban governments to increasingly appeal to the Crown and its provincial agents for support. Following Beaune's difficulties in collecting taxes in 1553, when plague struck again the following decade they obtained Charles IX's authorisation to impose a tax on the townspeople to help meet the costs of plague relief.[144] While the sum itself was small (233 *livres*), having Charles IX's written authorisation was important as anyone who refused to pay was disobeying a direct order from the monarch. Having the king's support was important because at the same time as the costs of plague care increased, normal municipal revenue streams declined. While Nevers' *échevins* struggled to cope with the costs of plague care in 1607, they also had to cut the annual sums they received from tax farmers, who were unable to collect normal levels of revenue because of the decimation of commercial activity. When the plague outbreak moved into 1608, the municipal council placed an extraordinary tax of 10,464 *livres* on the inhabitants to compensate for this reduction in ordinary revenue.[145] As the severity of plagues grew from the later sixteenth century, towns increasingly petitioned the Crown for financial support. In 1629, Louis XIII granted Nevers the right to levy a tax of 30,000 *livres* on the population for three years to meet the plague costs. As well as permitting the town council to raise such a large sum, the king also ruled that this was to apply to the town's clergy, which was important as they were traditionally exempt from urban taxation.[146]

Urban Communication Networks

While the increased involvement of the monarchy in the fight against plague helped to coordinate public health efforts across the kingdom, urban governments had long worked together to prevent the spread of the disease. Although towns designed and imposed their own set of plague regulations, they did not work in isolation. Municipal governments needed to cooperate for anti-plague systems to work effectively. Trust underpinned this system, which was based around the sharing of information. Urban governments informed their neighbours about the health of their own towns and passed on information

---

[143] AM Beaune Carton 88, no. 5, Carton 27, no. 16.   [144] AM Beaune Carton 23, no. 4.

[145] Boutillier, *Inventaire sommaire, Nevers*, pp. 78, 101.

[146] Boutillier, *Inventaire sommaire, Nevers*, p. 131.

about the progress of plague elsewhere, which we can clearly see when we examine the correspondence of Lyon's municipal council. Between 1556 and 1641, the city's government received news regarding the sanitary state of a wide range of towns, including: Aix-en-Provence, Arles, Augsburg, Avignon, Basel, Beaucaire, Belleville-sur-Saone, Bourg, Bourges, Chalons-sur-Saône, Chambéry, Clermont-Ferrand, Fribourg, Geneva, Grenoble, Heidelberg, Leipzig, Limoges, Lucerne, Marseille, Paris, Pont-Saint-Esprit, Riom, Roanne, Toulouse, Tours, Ulm, Valence, Vienne and Villefranche, many of whom they corresponded with directly. As we see, these information networks extended beyond France into Savoy (where they corresponded with both the ducal health council and the municipal council of Chambéry, capital of the duchy), Switzerland (Basel, Geneva, Lucerne) and Germany (Heidelberg, Leipzig, Ulm). The scale of their information gathering extended steadily over time. In 1602–4, they received news of the appearance of plague in Bruges, Calais, London and Lisbon.[147] Moreover, Lyon's *échevins* worked with their counterparts across political borders to help prevent the spread of plague. On the advice of the presence of plague at Basel in 1609, they worked with its town council to stop trade between the two cities.[148] Urban governments worked together on issues of common concern. In 1632, the *syndics* of Nice and Vence corresponded about the impact plague was having on commerce between the towns, while Avignon wrote to the *consuls* of Orange to stop receiving goods coming down the Rhône from Lyon, which was infected.[149]

As one of the most important commercial centres in the kingdom, Lyon was an information hub. In 1619, Avignon's *consuls* wrote to Lyon asking for news of plague in other parts of the kingdom.[150] Avignon then relayed information to its neighbours. In 1623, for instance, it informed Carpentras of the outbreak affecting northern cities, such as Amiens, Paris and Rouen.[151] Towns sought to provide as detailed information as they could about the severity of plague outbreaks to help others gauge the severity of the plague and whether it was increasing or decreasing. In 1637, Rodez learned that 160 houses in Lyon were closed up due to plague.[152] Even smaller towns could learn privileged information about plague outbreaks, which was then relayed to others. In October 1622, Avignon wrote to Salon asking for news of the outbreak which they had heard

---

[147] AM Lyon AA 66, 67, 72–3, 112, 114, 141.

[148] AM Lyon AA 156. For plague boundaries and Swiss cities, see: Eckert, 'Boundary Formation'.

[149] AM Nice GG 70/9; AD Vaucluse FRAD084_E Dépôt Avignon AA 18, fol. 184.

[150] AD Vaucluse FRAD084_E Dépôt Avignon AA 16, fols. 48, 49, AA 18, fols. 122, 180–180v, AA 20, fol. 163.

[151] AD Vaucluse FRAD084_E Dépôt Avignon AA 18, fol. 39.

[152] Affre, *Inventaire sommaire, Rodez*, p. 9.

had broken out at Martigues.[153] In 1611, Dijon's *échevins* informed Lyon that a merchant coming from Germany had brought plague to Lorraine and that Fontenay and eight or more surrounding villages were now infected.[154] This was important news for a commercial centre such as Lyon, which lay close to Lorraine.

Urban communication networks became especially important during the long and devastating plague which swept across Europe from the late 1620s. As plague entered southeastern France in late 1628, the volume of Avignon's correspondence increased considerably, as they maintained a steady stream of communication with its neighbours.[155] In August 1628 alone, Avignon's *consuls* wrote to their counterparts at Pierrelatte, Montélimar, Orange, Pont-St-Esprit, Montpellier, Valence, Vienne and Lyon, warning that they were placing restrictions on people and goods coming into Avignon and would only admit those with relevant health passports.[156] Once Avignon received confirmation that specific towns had succumbed to plague, it immediately implemented bans and informed the affected municipal governments.[157] The *consuls* also sent messages of support, such as that sent to Carpentras in December 1628 expressing their condolences that the plague had taken hold there.[158]

Urban governments needed to be sure that the information they received from other towns was accurate and given honestly, as it had a direct effect on the actions they took. Rather than delay implementing plague measures (as French towns are often accused of doing), municipal councils were generally diligent and sought to take action early, as it was more preferable to try and prevent plague from entering than to wait for an outbreak to take hold. As soon as Rodez learned that disease was present in the villages of Nant and Saint-Jean-du-Breul, despite lying over 80 km away they immediately began to take preventative measures.[159] In June 1616, Avignon wrote to Aix-en-Provence to inform them that there was no need for concern about the anti-plague measures being implemented in Montélimar as there was no plague there. Rather, they were being initiated as a precaution against plague coming from Geneva, where there was a bad outbreak.[160] Information received from

---

[153] AD Vaucluse FRAD084_E Dépôt Avignon AA 17, fol. 114.   [154] AM Lyon AA 157.

[155] These were: Pierrelatte, Montélimar, Orange, Pont-St-Esprit, Montpellier, Valence, Lyon, Aix, Carpentras, Tarascon, Vienne, Arles, Marseille, Toulon, Pont-St Esprit, Beaucaire, Roquemare, Nimes and Uzès.

[156] AD Vaucluse FRAD084_E Dépôt Avignon AA 18, fols. 169–72.

[157] AD Vaucluse FRAD084_E Dépôt Avignon AA 18, fol. 175.

[158] AD Vaucluse FRAD084_E Dépôt Avignon AA 20, fol. 12.

[159] Affre, *Inventaire sommaire, Rodez*, p. 9.

[160] AD Vaucluse FRAD084_E Dépôt Avignon AA 15, fol. 97.

neighbouring towns also caused urban leaders to lift restrictions. When Lyon informed Grenoble in August 1520 that it had been a long time since any plague death was recorded in the city, Grenoble's *consuls* raised the trade interdiction with the city.[161] Larger towns could see themselves as protectors for their smaller neighbours. On 23 September 1628, Bordeaux's *jurade*, learning of the presence of plague at Lyon, advised their 'god-daughter towns' (*villes filleules*) to protect themselves against the plague.[162] If towns were unsure about the information they received they could check with their neighbours. In September 1681, upon rumours of the presence of plague at Perpignan, St Pons' town council sent a messenger to Narbonne to check with its *consuls*.[163] In contrast to Italian states, there is little evidence of French towns making extensive use of spies to report on their neighbours during plague times.[164] For the most part, they worked on a system of mutual trust and we find the regular and open sharing of information between communities.

Plague in the Countryside

As well as communicating with neighbouring towns, urban governments monitored surrounding villages for plague because the countryside was a main source of infection. Already in 1420, Saint-Flour was instructing residents of infected villages to stay away (though despite these precautions it was infected by people from the village of Traverges), while at Rodez in June 1460 the town council first noted the presence of plague in the villages of Saint-Geniez-d'Olt and Mur-de-Barrez.[165] The French countryside remained a key source of infection throughout the early modern period. In 1623, Laon's municipal council implemented measures 'to protect this city and suburbs as far as possible from the contagious evil of the plague which is said to be in the surrounding places and villages'.[166] Lyon's *échevins* monitored villages in the surrounding region and corresponded regularly with them to check for plague.[167] This was with good reason as the devastating outbreak which hit the city in 1628 came from the village of Vaux-en-Beaujolais, reputedly by soldiers returning from Italy.[168] In Lorraine, villages were devastated in the plague of the 1630s and thirty-seven were totally abandoned.[169] At Sanzey, 'the said village is completely deserted and ruined, there are no inhabitants, all of

---

[161] AM Grenoble BB 5, fol. 18v.
[162] Boisville, *Registres de la Jurade, Bordeaux*, vol. I, p. 532.
[163] AD Hérault, 284 EDT 26, fol. 9.   [164] Carmichael, 'Contagion Theory', p. 519.
[165] Boudet and Grand, *Documents inédits*, pp. 46–7 ; Affre, *Inventaire sommaire, Rodez*, p. 2.
[166] Matton, *Inventaire sommaire, Laon*, p. 97.   [167] AM Lyon AA 48.
[168] Canard, *Pestes*, p. 146 ; AM Lyon AA 118.   [169] Le Page, 'Dépopulation en Lorraine'.

whom are dead or refugees in Toul', while at Mont-le Vignoble there was nobody left except 'two or three poor inhabitants and two widows; the rest amongst the world, begging for their life'.[170] The evidence from the *Chambre de comptes* of Lorraine highlights the devastating effect which plagues had on the countryside in the duchy between the 1540s and the 1630s.[171] Plague continued to affect French villages badly right through to the 1720s, with La Valette-du-Var in Provence losing almost two-thirds of its population during the outbreak.[172] It could devastate even very remote villages. In the 1560s, Rodez took measures to protect itself from an outbreak of plague in the villages of Espalion, Cabrespine and Les Bessades in the sparsely populated hills north of the town.[173] Overall, then, an examination of the countryside shows a persistent level of infection within France throughout the early modern period, which stands at odds with the narrative of early modern plague being overwhelmingly an urban disease.

It was important to identify infectious diseases which struck villages, as towns implemented special measures for plague. In 1613, Nevers sent its plague surgeon to visit individuals in the surrounding villages of Baratte and Imphy suffering from an unidentified contagious disease.[174] When the consuls of Albi learned in 1630 that disease had infected the nearby small town of Tanus, they sent two physicians and a surgeon to confirm that it was plague, as part of which they were instructed to exhume the corpses of the recent dead. As soon as these medical experts confirmed that it was plague, the *consuls* wrote to neighbouring villages and small towns not to admit anyone from Tanus or bringing goods along the river Tarn.[175] Early modern towns were concerned about river traffic, as this was a principal route for trade. When Bordeaux's *jurade* learned in 1628 that plague was present in the villages of the *Haut-Pays* of Gascony, they prohibited communication with these settlements and placed a boat filled with armed men in the Garonne to stop any vessels from the high country from reaching the city.[176]

As well as spreading plague to towns, villages could remain infected long after the eradication of urban outbreaks. Accordingly, municipal governments needed to continue to monitor surrounding villages to ensure that they did not

---

[170] Bouchot, 'Peste de Lorraine', pp. 156–8.

[171] AD Meurthe-et-Moselle B 1027, B 1076, B 1081, B 1146, B 1147, B 1149, B 1151, B 1924, B 1581, B 2133, B 2346, B 5149, B 5385, B 5451, B 5433, B 5714, B 6188, B 6210, B 6592, B 6659, B 6693, B 6951, B 6757.

[172] Buti, *Peste à La Valette*, p. 8.   [173] Affre, *Inventaire sommaire, Rodez*, p. 7.

[174] Boutillier, *Inventaire sommaire, Nevers*, p. 105. See also for Auch in 1678: AD Gers 1Édépôt BB 6, fol. 642v.

[175] Vidal, 'Peste d'Albi', p. 173.

[176] Boisville, *Registres de la Jurade, Bordeaux*, vol. I, p. 532.

reinfect the city. While a bad outbreak of plague had subsided at Grenoble by late 1524, it remained present in surrounding villages. In March 1525, the *consuls* noted that it still raged in the remote Alpine villages of La Buissière, Goncelin and Allevard and Gières.[177] As such, they immediately reissued their plague regulations to try and prevent reinfection. It was only because urban governments had good systems in place to monitor the sanitary state of villages that such instances came to their attention early, thus allowing them time to act to try and prevent plague from reaching them. When in 1561 Auch's municipal council saw that plague was present in the neighbouring villages of Gimont, L'Isle and Mauzevin, they closed their gates and established an extramural building where anyone seeking entry to the town first had to quarantine.[178] As plague infected villages throughout Quércy in 1631, Rodez immediately implemented its plague regulations. One of the infected locations was Carjac, which was a stop on the route to Santiago de Compostela; this raises the possibility of rural areas becoming infected through pilgrimages.[179]

Municipal governments alerted the governments of other towns about the presence of plague in villages, so that they too could take the necessary precautions. It was in their benefit to alert their neighbours because the worse the plague got the more chance there was of them getting infected. Moreover, they could demonstrate that they were healthy and doing all they could to remain so. In 1628, Avignon's *consuls* wrote to those of neighbouring Tarascon to advise that they were carefully guarding the town from suspected villages in the surrounding area, particularly Baume, Bédoin, Vacqueyras, Lafare and Loriol.[180] They also kept in contact with healthy villages to help them avoid infection. When news of plague reached Narbonne in September 1591, the *consuls* immediately wrote to the surrounding villages advising them to avoid all contact with foreigners.[181] The fact that this was the first act taken by the municipal council highlights that they understood that the health of town and countryside were closely linked.

Historians often stress a dichotomy between the rural and urban experiences of natural disasters such as plague. François Lebrun writes that 'the inequality between cities and the countryside is flagrant: in times of famine or plague, rural

---

[177] AM Grenoble, BB 8, fol. 83v. Certainly, this had happened before. At Grenoble in March 1523, just a few months after the town has been declared free of plague in December 1522, the town council announced that a man has died from plague at the village of Saint-Martin-le-Vinoux, and the city itself was soon reinfected: AM Grenoble, BB 8, fol. 41.

[178] AD Gers 1Édépôt BB 5, fol. 89v.

[179] It had reached villages immediately surrounding Rodez, including Villecomtal, 20km to the north: Affre, *Inventaire sommaire, Rodez*, p. 8.

[180] AD Vaucluse FRAD084_E Dépôt Avignon AA 18, fol. 191; AA 19, fols. 1–2.

[181] AM Narbonne BB 5, fol. 388.

populations are left to fend for themselves'.[182] Yet French municipal councils regularly sent support to village communities. As early as 1420, Saint-Flour paid a woman (probably a local village healer) to treat the infected of the village of Carlat.[183] When Lyon's *échevins* learned that plague had broken out in the neighbouring village of Tarare in April 1531, they immediately raised funds to send to help the infected.[184] There was undoubtedly a strong degree of municipal self-interest in such actions. As villages were a leading source of infection for towns, it was desirable to help them remain healthy. In 1518, Laon sent a delegation to visit a house in the neighbouring village of Bousson which was infected with plague. They also paid for the victuals of the infected to prevent them from coming to town ('affin de ne converser en ladicte ville').[185] In the 1680s, Aix-en-Provence paid neighbouring coastal villages and small towns the costs they incurred of quarantining sailors who came from infected places.[186]

While the evidence is less complete than that for urban areas, the information we have about rural plague in France suggests that villages could have developed plague-care systems. For instance, Saint Aubin-de-Scellon in Normandy had a building that was being used as a plague hospital or quarantine centre, while the small town of Chazay-d'Azergues, which lay on the Rhône, also had a plague hospital. Indeed, the village of Condrieu, which lay 60 km downriver from Chazy, may have had a hospital run by the clergy specifically for plague victims as early as 1348.[187] In 1589, one resident of the lordship of Tigéville in the duchy of Lorraine was fined for having disobeyed an order from a sergeant to go to the lodges used to place the plague sick, which suggests that there were both quarantine centres and an enforcement system operating in the countryside.[188] As the authority of urban health boards did not extend beyond the *banlieue* (the rural parts surrounding a town which were directly under municipal jurisdiction), they worked with royal officials in the countryside. At Troyes, the royal officers of the surrounding *bailliage* organised local lords to oversee and pay for plague care in the countryside, including bringing in physicians and surgeons, while deputies from infected villages liaised with the town council and health board regarding the implementation of plague regulations. In each village a man was named to organise victuals for infected houses and those who had communication with the sick were instructed to call out to warn people to stay away until they reached their houses, where they were

[182] Lebrun, 'Intervention', p. 39.   [183] Boudet and Grand, *Documents inédits*, p. 45.
[184] Rolland and Clouzet, *Communes*, vol. II, p. 544.
[185] Matton, *Inventaire sommaire, Laon*, p. 13.   [186] AM Aix-en-Provence CC 390, no. 44.
[187] Fournée, *Normands*, p. 45 ; Rolland and Clouzet, *Communes*, vol. I, pp. 139, 174.
[188] AD Meurthe-et-Moselle B 2346.

to stay unless they 'retired to the huts in the field', again showing that there was a quarantine system in place in rural areas.[189]

As well as providing help, urban governments took punitive actions to prevent plague spreading out of villages. In 1666, when physicians in the employ of Amiens' municipal council confirmed that many people had died from plague in the nearby village of Dury, they had the village isolated.[190] Avignon's *consuls* enclosed all suspected villages in the surrounding region and forbade them from having outside contact for a period of three weeks.[191] Such actions were to a large degree dependent on urban governments having jurisdiction over surrounding areas, which many did not as French *banlieues* were typically much smaller than the hinterlands of Italian or Spanish towns. In these circumstances, they barred their gates to specific villages. When plague was found at the village of Rémi outside of Compiègne in 1520, the municipal council paid a guard 'in order to prevent the inhabitants of Rémi, where they were dying of the plague, from entering the town'.[192] The rulers of Verdun attached lists of villages of which the inhabitants were forbidden entry to the town under pain of death, while one man and three women from the infected village of Saint-Mauds who were caught bringing goods to Troyes in 1531 were publicly beaten.[193]

As *parlements* took over the issuing of plague ordinances during the sixteenth century, they included villages within the provisions. The ordinances issued by the *parlement* of Burgundy in 1597 included regulations relating to entry into villages and the obtaining of health certificates (from the parish priest) as well as warning the villagers not to 'disguise or conceal their place of residence on pain of being shot'.[194] Royal authorities worked with municipal councils to help prevent plague spreading from the countryside into urban centres. As plague was spreading across northeastern France in 1666, it reached villages surrounding Amiens by early summer. To prevent it from infecting the city, the royal officials of the *bailliage* issued an ordinance forbidding the villages from trading with the city. This ruling was given further weight a month later when the *parlement* of Paris issued an order confirming this prohibition (though with exemptions for those who had bills of health).[195] Then the *indendant* (the most powerful royal official in the provinces by the mid-seventeenth century) used his authority to help the town council by placing an officer in each infected

---

[189] Boutiot, *Pestes de Troyes*, pp. 35–6.   [190] AM Amiens GG 1132.
[191] AD Vaucluse FRAD084_E Dépôt Avignon AA 18, fol. 191 ; AA 19, fols. 1–2.
[192] AM Compiègne CC 37, fol. 212.
[193] Bouchot, 'Peste de Lorraine', p. 147 ; Boutiot, *Pestes de Troyes*, p. 30. See also : Boutillier, *Inventaire sommaire, Nevers*, p. 50 ; Matton, *Inventaire sommaire, Laon*, p. 93.
[194] Garnier (ed.), *Journal de Gabriel Breunot*, vol. III, p. 95.   [195] AM Amiens GG 1130.

village to ensure that the villagers obeyed the plague regulations.[196] Again, we see multiple authorities (municipal council, *parlement*, *indendant*, *bailliage*) working together to prevent the spread of plague.

Clergy

Beyond working with outside institutions, municipal councils liaised with the local clergy. There is little work on the role the clergy played in plague relief in pre-modern France, with discussions tending to focus on a few well-known figures such as the actions of Henri-François Xavier de Belsunce, bishop of Marseille, who personally tended to the sick in the 1720s.[197] Yet the clergy were essential in two main areas: (1) helping pay for plague relief and (2) caring for the infected. Beyond seeking authorisation from the king or *parlement* to raise the taxes, municipal councils utilised the support of the clergy to encourage townspeople to contribute to plague relief. When Narbonne's *consuls* wanted to build a plague hospital in 1546, they appealed to the clergy and the cathedral chapter, as well as wealthy townspeople.[198] Having the assistance of the clergy was helpful because employing parish structures was a highly effective way to communicate with townspeople and organise collections. At Rouen in 1562, the costs of plague led the town council to publish instructions in each parish stating that they would make door-to-door collections for gifts, with the townspeople being encouraged to donate as a mark of devotion.[199] Again in 1581, Rouen's parish priests gave sermons on behalf of the town council encouraging their parishioners to make gifts to help with the plague support.[200] During the plague outbreak at Narbonne in the early 1630s, the town council installed a committee to work with the clergy and decide parish by parish who were permitted to remain (native poor) and who were to be expelled (foreign poor).[201]

The clergy were also key to the material and spiritual care of the sick. When the barber-surgeons of Beauvais refused to treat the sick in 1520, the Franciscans took over.[202] Members of religious orders were increasingly keen to serve in plague hospitals from the later sixteenth century. Tending to the sick – and especially the poor sick – was a key manifestation of Counter-Reformation piety. However, as plague care increasingly became the preserve of physicians and surgeons, the clergy focused on the spiritual needs of their patients.[203] Prayer was used in combination with medical procedures, such as

---

[196] AM Amiens GG 1135.

[197] For Belsunce, see: Praviel, *Belsunce*; Bérenger (ed.), *Journal*; Bertrand, *Belsunce*.

[198] AM Narbonne BB 1, fol. 282v.   [199] AD Seine-Maritime 3^E 1 Rouen AA 18, fol. 126v.

[200] AD Seine-Maritime 3^E 1 Rouen AA 20, fol. 98.   [201] AM Narbonne BB 18, fol. 153.

[202] Rose, *Inventaire sommaire, Beauvais*, p. 16.

[203] Boisville, *Registres de la Jurade, Bordeaux*, vol. I, p. 547.

bloodletting, to treat plague. During the plague outbreak at Nevers in 1530, the town council paid a priest to confess and administer the sacrament to the infected.[204] Similarly, when the Parisians constructed a large permanent plague hospital at Grenelle in 1580, they employed a team of clergy to be constantly available for the plague victims.[205]

Some health boards had the power to appoint clergy, such as that installed at Narbonne in 1580 which named two priests to confess the plague sick.[206] Yet, given the dangers of tending to the infected, clergy could also be reluctant to serve in plague hospitals, which posed a particular problem for town councils as their authority did not extend over the clergy. Given the essential role that the clergy played in plague care, urban governments appealed to regional sources of royal authority to compel them to tend to the sick. When Rouen set up a plague hospital in 1580, the town council petitioned the city's royal lieutenant to instruct the clergy 'to administer the sacraments to the sick and to confess them'.[207] In 1634, Amiens' *échevins* asked the *parlement* of Paris to order the clergy to administer to the sick, some of whom were dying without having received the sacraments because the clergy were refusing to enter the same space as the infected.[208] Again it was the combination of authorities which led to the implementation of holistic plague care that looked to both the physical and spiritual needs of the sick.

***

By the mid-sixteenth century, French towns had developed comprehensive anti-plague systems. Yet municipal councils are often accused of failing to act or of dereliction of duty. For S. Annette Finley-Croswhite, during times of plague '[urban] governments collapsed and lawlessness prevailed after the town notables fled', while Jacques Revel argues that in terms of municipal authority 'it is often anarchy' due to the flight of urban leaders.[209] While we can find occasional examples of urban governments collapsing, these are rare by the sixteenth century and on the whole municipal councils responded quickly and diligently to the crisis. At Auch in 1630 the council decided to meet regularly on Tuesday and Friday each week at 7am until the end of the plague as soon as they heard of the first death.[210] In both 1522 and 1587, several members of Beauvais' municipal council died while overseeing the implementation of plague

---

[204] Boutillier, *Inventaire sommaire, Nevers*, p. 53. See also : Boisville, *Registres de la Jurade, Bordeaux*, vol. I, p. 526.

[205] Guérin (ed.), *Registres des délibérations, Paris, 1539–1552*, p. 228.

[206] AM Narbonne BB 5, fol. 408v.   [207] AD Seine-Maritime 3E1 AA 20, fol. 101v.

[208] AM Amiens BB 63, fol. 16v.

[209] Finley-Croswhite, *Henry IV*, pp. 16–17; Revel, 'Épidémie ancienne', pp. 966, 969.

[210] AD Gers 1Edépôt Auch BB 6, fol. 341.

regulations.[211] When plague struck Castres in 1595 amongst those killed were many members of the ruling elite of the town, including *consuls*.[212] Indeed, it was typically town councils who acted most vigorously to try and prevent flight. François Lebrun writes that in Breton towns 'most of the *échevins* [aldermen] and municipal officers fled like the others' during outbreaks, despite the fact that towns across Brittany put sophisticated plague systems in place during the early modern period.[213]

Beyond the individual efforts of civic governments, we find a high degree of cooperation between towns. Municipal leaders corresponded with each other, sharing information and expertise. Big cities acted as communication centres and their rulers shared information about the national picture with their smaller neighbours. We also saw that towns were strongly connected to the countryside and were in constant dialogue with villages, whether that be in terms of seeking out information, providing medical support or communicating travel restrictions. Long before the Crown took over the coordination of information between communities, town governments were already doing this, working in networks which extended across the kingdom and beyond. We also got a glimpse of how urban governments were supported by the monarchy and its provincial representatives, which will be examined in more detail in the following section.

4 The Crown and Plague

On 13 September 1669, in the midst of the major plague outbreak affecting northern France, Louis XIV wrote to Dieppe's municipal council instructing them to follow the advice of the royal doctor he had sent to the town and to 'punctually observe the police orders [i.e. the plague regulations]', 'assuring you that on our part, we will give you all the help that we can'.[214] In this letter, Louis XIV neatly set out the three key elements of the Bourbon monarchy's plague policy. Namely, that urban governments – who continued to take the lead in the war against plague – were to ensure that the plague ordinances they had been largely responsible for devising in the previous century were observed rigorously, particularly in terms of keeping the infected separate from the sick (and preferably placed in a plague hospital). In terms of medical treatments, the king and his physicians were asserting ultimate sanction over the form of medical treatments, especially the disinfection methods used on people, homes and goods. And finally, that the Crown would provide material support to embattled towns, which included both extending their powers and providing

---

[211] Rose, *Inventaire sommaire, Beauvais*, p. 25.   [212] Estadieu, *Castres*, pp. 60, 70.
[213] Lebrun, 'Intervention', p. 43.   [214] Guibert, *Dieppe*, vol. II, p. 39.

money. Yet the monarch was only one element in this scheme and a range of other Crown authorities worked with municipal councils to develop a polycentric plague management system.

Parlements

As the principal legislative bodies in the provinces, *parlements* gave legal weight to plague ordinances and enforced standardised measures across a wide area. In 1628, the ordinances of the *parlement* of Provence covered a range of issues concerning plague, from the disinfection of goods to the holding of religious ceremonies.[215] In these texts, *parlements* declared that the instructions applied to all those in their jurisdictions, including royal officials and the clergy, authority over whom typically lay beyond the remit of municipal governments.[216] *Parlements* were representatives of king and they acted in his name. In August 1628, the *parlement* of Dauphiné issued plague orders 'by the king and the authority of our lords of the Court of the *parlement* of Dauphiné'.[217] Rather than supplanting municipal authority, *parlements* worked closely with town councils and lent them their authority to help enforce anti-plague measures. Indeed, it was municipal councils who first reached out to *parlements* in the early sixteenth century to seek their support. In the 1520s, Grenoble's municipal council approached the *parlement* of Dauphiné with various requests for help regarding plague, seeking its help on matters that lay outside of municipal jurisdiction. They wanted the *parlement* to stop soldiers entering the town (out of fear that they would bring the disease with them) and to accelerate the judgements of those imprisoned in the city, as plague had infected the jail. In January 1526, they asked the *parlement* to quicken the judgement on a woman named Guillemette, then pregnant, who was part of a band of criminals believed to have introduced the plague into the town (the others had already been condemned to death).[218]

Although the *parlements* took over the issuing of plague ordinances in many parts of France during the mid-sixteenth century, they did little to innovate. Rather, they took measures devised by urban groups and standardised them and then imposed them across their jurisdictions. For instance, the extensive set of plague regulations the *parlement* of Paris issued in 1533 was composed in consultation with the municipal council and the *prévôt* of Paris.[219] *Parlements* used their legal authority to help the town overcome many of the difficulties they encountered in enforcing plague regulations. In October 1592, when the *parlement* of Rouen first learned of deaths from plague, it immediately issued plague ordinances and tasked

---

[215] BNF Dupuy 659, fols. 164–6.   [216] See: AM Amiens GG 1136.
[217] AM Grenoble AA 23.   [218] AM Grenoble BB 6, fol. 382, BB 8, fols. 27, 203.
[219] *Edicts et ordonnances des roys de France*, pp. 1061–4 ; Essarts, *Dictionnaire universel de police*, vol. III, pp. 216–17. For the Parisian ordinances, see: Chéreau, *Ordonnances*.

the municipal council with implementing them. The *parlement* then worked closely with the *échevins* to combat the outbreak, lending them their authority when needed. In January 1669, the *parlement* of Normandy forbade the transport of goods outside Rouen and the councillors launched legal trials against those who broke this instruction.[220] As we saw in the previous section, preventing fleeing elites taking goods – and especially foodstuffs – was a key problem facing municipal councils, especially as it could lead to sedition. Obtaining supplies was another key difficulty facing urban governments. In 1650, the *parlement* of Provence ordered that all medicines in Aix-en-Provence were to be handed over to the town council so that they could be given to those infected with plague.[221] The closest relationships developed between *parlements* and the elites of the cities in which they sat, particularly Aix-en-Provence, Bordeaux, Dijon, Grenoble, Paris, Rouen and Toulouse. *Parlements* also sent agents out to report on the situations in other infected towns in their jurisdictions. In 1668, for instance, the *parlement* of Paris sent Chrétien-Français de Lamoignon to report on the outbreak at Soissons.[222] Yet even here cooperation between *parlements* and their chief cities was crucial as the inspector which the *parlement* of Paris sent to the surrounding area was the Parisian *échevin*, Belin, who had the power to give orders to local authorities in the *parlement*'s jurisdiction, including other urban governments, such as that of Mantes.[223]

We can clearly see this relationship between a *parlement* and a municipal council when we examine relations between the *parlement* of Bordeaux and the civic administration during the outbreaks which occurred in the city between the mid-sixteenth and mid-seventeenth centuries. While the *parlement* contributed to plague relief in the city from the mid-sixteenth century, it was the severe plague of 1585–6 which brought it to the forefront of the implementation of anti-plague legislation.[224] From this date the *parlement* rather than the city council issued the plague ordinances, though the *jurade* remained responsible for putting plague measures (which they had devised) into operation.[225] As the jurisdiction of the municipal council was limited to the city and its immediate surroundings, the *parlement*'s orders imposed Bordeaux's regulations on all communities across the province. This worked considerably to the council's advantage, especially as it helped prevent people from infected places from coming to the city. Furthermore, the *parlement* also helped the city raise funds for anti-plague measures. In July 1585, it both contributed its own funds and allowed a new plague tax to be placed on the townspeople. When the plague

---

[220] BNF Mélanges Colbert 150, fols. 803–22.   [221] AM Aix-en-Provence BB 143, fol. 1.

[222] BNF Français 9557, fols. 171–206.   [223] Trout, 'Plague of 1668', pp. 418–19.

[224] Boisville, *Registres de la Jurade,* vol. I, p. 527.

[225] Boisville, *Registres de la Jurade,* vol. I, pp. 527–8.

finally subsided in late 1586, the *parlement* issued letters patent allowing the city council to continue to levy taxes to pay for the deficit plague care had left in the budget (and it also provided further money itself). These measures saved the town from bankruptcy.[226] Other *parlements* took similar actions. In March 1577, Dijon approached the *parlement* of Burgundy asking for its support both in having the tax of 10,000 *livres* the king had placed on the town reduced and helping them raise the money they needed 'for the great expenses it suited them to bear because of the plague sick'.[227] Then during the outbreak in the later 1590s, the *parlement* of Burgundy decided to triple the annual sum they gave for the support of the poor 'to provide for the plague sick and those of the city [Dijon]'.[228]

The transfer in authority to the *parlement* of Bordeaux of the implementation of plague measures meant that when the *jurade* feared that a new outbreak of the disease was about to strike the city in December 1612, they sent a delegation to the *parlement* to ask for its permission to renew the plague ordinances.[229] As we see, it was the town who was proactive and took the initiative to implement anti-plague measures before the disease struck the town, rather than the *parlement* having to force a reluctant municipal council to act. In October 1628, as plague again drew closer to the city, the town council sent a delegation to the *parlement* informing them that people and goods from infected towns in Languedoc were preparing to come to Bordeaux, for which they asked the councillors to use their authority to stop this. In response, the *parlement* immediately issued orders forbidding people or goods from infected places in Languedoc from entering any territory in its jurisdiction. Moreover, they also prohibited all residents of Aquitaine from receiving people or goods from infected regions. Anyone who wished to trade with Bordeaux first had to spend time in a quarantine centre under penalty of death. It was the wider authority which the *parlement* possessed over the region which was crucial in helping Bordeaux's *jurats* try to stop the disease from taking hold in their city, in which respect the provincial governor also came to play a role.

Governors

The sixteenth century also saw the rise of the provincial governors, who represented the king in the provinces.[230] Like the *parlements*, they possessed wide-ranging powers which saw them become involved in the management of

---

[226] Boisville, *Registres de la Jurade,* vol. I, p. 528.

[227] Garnier (ed.), *Journal de Gabriel Breunot,* vol. I, p. 198.

[228] Garnier (ed.), *Journal de Gabriel Breunot,* vol. I, p. 186.

[229] For the following two paragraphs, see: Boisville, *Registres de la Jurade,* vol. I, pp. 529, 532, 535–6, 547–8, 550–1.

[230] Barbiche, *Monarchie française,* p. 323.

plague-control measures, though this aspect of their authority has not been examined.[231] Like the *parlements* and other agents of the Crown, the governors did little to innovate in terms of disease-control measures. Moreover, they tended to support municipal councils. During the plague outbreak at Bordeaux in 1629–32, the city council sent regular reports to Jean-Louis de Nogaret de La Valette, governor of Guyenne, detailing the sanitary state of the town. They asked for his help in ways that drew on his powers. For instance, they asked La Valette to stop soldiers in the surrounding region harassing the population and to use his personal standing as one of the most important men in France to secure the provision of grain for the city.[232] Both these actions were of vital importance during a plague outbreak, when securing provisions became a pressing issue for town councils.

As with *parlements*, urban governments sought to employ a governor's authority to help them enforce plague regulations. In 1631, the *parlement* of Guyenne gave Limoges' *consuls* the right to levy a plague tax on the population to help meet plague costs. When this was met with opposition and people refused to pay, the governor helped the town council enforce the ruling.[233] At Troyes during the bad outbreak of 1521, when the town was attracting large number of poor refugees, the governor of Champagne issued an order saying that all non-native poor had to leave the town within a day or else they would be whipped and driven out, while in 1529 he used his authority to maintain a food supply for the city, especially with regard to grain coming from surrounding areas.[234] At Angers in 1629, the governor forbade inhabitants of the town (under pain of a fine of 100 *livres*) to go to infected parishes in the countryside.[235] As we saw in the previous section, preventing people from leaving the town was a key concern for municipal councils, as was avoiding contact with infected rural areas.

As well as helping municipal councils enforce plague regulations, by the seventeenth century – and especially from the 1630s – the monarch used governors to monitor outbreaks of plague and report on the actions of urban governments. This represented a key moment in the evolution of the monarchy's involvement in the management of plague outbreaks. We clearly see both these aspects of governors' actions when we examine relations between Honoré d'Albret, duke of Chaulnes and governor of Picardy, and Amiens during the severe outbreak which afflicted the city in the 1630s. From the very beginning of the outbreak right through to its cessation, Chaulnes worked closely with the

---

[231] For the key study of the provincial governors, see: Harding, *Power Elite*.

[232] Coste, 'Bordeaux et la peste', pp. 465–6.

[233] Ruben (ed.), *Registres consulaires*, vol. III, pp. 277–8.

[234] Boutiot, *Pestes de Troyes*, pp. 24, 27.   [235] David, *Peste à Angers*, p. 44.

town council in all matters concerning plague.[236] Chaulnes was often at court in Paris throughout the outbreak, so the town kept a representative there to promote the needs and affairs of the city relating to plague with him.[237] In January 1635, for instance, they had their representative appeal for assistance to Chalunes for help with the massive debts they had accumulated because of the plague.[238] In November 1633, he wrote to the town council that he was departing for the court and would advocate for them in Paris, saying 'I will make known to the king the care you take in the exercise of your duties, for the preservation of his people, so that, contributing to it with some manifestation of his goodness [i.e. practical help such as tax remissions], he always gives you courage to do well and to act well'.[239]

It was a two-way street and as well as promoting urban interests at court, governors relayed measures from the centre to the provinces. During a visit to Paris in 1623, Chaulnes wrote to Amiens with news of the outbreak in the capital and an account of the measures the Parisian municipal council were using.[240] As well as being useful for the town council, it furthered the Bourbon monarchy's aim of having Paris, the principal focus for monarchical efforts with regard to plague, act as a model for other towns. In 1628, Chaulnes inspected the designs the town proposed for a new plague hospital and visited the intended site of the building. Louis XIII's policy at this time was to take the royal plague hospital his father founded at Paris in 1607 as the model and to have other cities establish new buildings which followed this design. Certainly, the design Chaulnes approved at Amiens was based on that of the Saint-Louis plague hospital.[241]

Although the town council welcomed Chaulnes' involvement in this construction of a new plague hospital, other attempts to enforce royal policy regarding plague measures brought him into conflict with the town council. When the town's physicians and a faction of townspeople opposed the methods used by one Henry Le Cointe, an *aireur* (a person who disinfected goods and homes) operating in Amiens with royal backing, and sought to drive him out, Chaulnes declared that these actions were 'detrimental to the service of the king and the rest of the public'. In response, Chaulnes declared that the *aireur* (who had been threatened with violence) was under his special protection and that he would act personally against anyone who attacked him. It was during this period that the king and his physicians were taking closer involvement in the medical methods used against the plague and seeking to encourage the use of royally approved treatments in the provinces. While this faction of townspeople and the

[236] AM Amiens BB 63, fol. 97v.
[237] AM Amiens BB 62, fols. 259v, 292v; AM Amiens AA 61.   [238] AM Amiens AA 60
[239] AM Amiens AA 59.   [240] AM Amiens BB 61, fols. 118, 199.
[241] AM Amiens BB 61, fols. 198v–199r, 201r, 222v.

physicians had good cause to be concerned about the *aireur* (particularly that he was using arsenic in his treatments), nonetheless his methods had royal backing and he had employed them, apparently successfully, in other towns.[242]

The concerns about Le Cointe also perhaps represented a wider dissatisfaction about the strict implementation of quarantine the monarchy favoured. In the sixteenth century, Amiens like other northern towns (and indeed those in places such as Spain, the Low Countries and Piedmont) had favoured a looser implementation of these methods. In the 1590s, Henry IV had instructed the towns of the northeast to enforce stricter quarantine than they had been doing and now with severe plague hitting again in the 1630s there still seemed to be some residual preference for the older, looser scheme, which allowed controlled circulation of the sick in the streets, provided they carried a white stick. We see a resurgence of these ideas in other northern towns during the plague of the 1620s/30s. At Chartres in 1629, the town council ruled that the sick needed to isolate in their homes, but that one member of each household could 'with a white stick, buy their goods' between 8am and 9am and again between 4pm and 5pm.[243]

It was by 1634, when the plague had already been in Amiens for several years, that we find the resurgence of these older methods, probably because the plague had still not disappeared. Nonetheless, Chaulnes, possibly correctly, tied this laxness in observing the regulations to the resurgence of the plague in the city. He accused the town council of mismanagement by failing to enforce the plague ordinances, stating that the city 'is threatened with utter ruin' and that 'all the evil comes from the bad policing'. He was particularly concerned that the infected were remaining in the city and not going to the extramural plague hospital, of which, as we have seen, he had approved the design in the previous decade. He first sought to help the town council enforce the regulations by instructing the sick to go to the plague hospital or else face a fine of 1,000 *livres*, an enormous sum, which also suggests that it was the wealthy who were disobeying the plague regulations.[244] Other towns across France were also struggling with the implementation of strict quarantine. The physician at Villefranche-de-Rouergue noted in 1629 the 'insolence and bad behaviour committed by some of the plague sick'.[245] When Amiens' town council was still unable to enforce the plague regulations, Chaulnes threatened to 'impose

---

[242] He had also treated plague sick at Calais, Dunkirk, Nice and Soissons. In Nice's municipal registers, he is called *médicin du roi*, though it is not clear that he had any formal medical training (Amiens's doctors call him a 'so-called surgeon'): AM Nice GG 70/5; Malpart, *Peste à Amiens*, pp. 33–41; Revel, 'Autour', p. 63.

[243] Cited in: Lebrun, 'Intervention', p. 41.   [244] AM Amiens AA 60.

[245] Foucault and Mouysset, 'Ordre et desordre', p. 24.

a greater authority, and that I will resort to violent remedies'. He told the *échevins* 'I want violence to be used even to the point of demolishing and setting fire to houses; that if you do not do it at once, I will ask the king for one or two regiments to put in the city, and make the soldiers do, by the command of His Majesty, what you do not do in your charges'.[246] Yet the problem was not that the town council was unwilling to enforce the regulations, but that they lacked the resources to do so over a reluctant population who had lived with four years of restrictions. Given the difficulties in enforcing plague measures, towns often welcomed the use of soldiers to help them maintain order.

Soldiers

While Chaulnes threatened to deploy soldiers on Amiens, it was normally towns who petitioned governors for military support during plague outbreaks. It is indicative of the difficulties urban governments faced in imposing plague regulations that they called for the support of soldiers, who, along with the poor, were frequently identified as the principal carriers of the disease (a stereotype reinforced by the fact that common soldiers often came from the poorer classes) and who also caused wider infractions against civilians during outbreaks.[247] The decree the *parlement* of Normandy issued in October 1623 regarding a plague outbreak, which had made three–quarters of Lisieux 'almost deserted', noted the misery caused by 'strangers, soldiers and vagabonds, who ordinarily arrive here with the intention of plundering not only the houses of the absent, but also afflicting them with the same contagion'.[248]

We see the tensions between trying to restrict the movements of soldiers on one hand and seeking their support during bad outbreaks when we examine the actions of Narbonne's municipal council in the 1590s. Learning of the presence of plague in the surrounding region in September 1591, Narbonne's *consuls* sent a delegation to the duke of Joyeuse, governor of the town, asking him to prevent soldiers from his army, which was camped nearby, from coming to the town. Should he want provisions, they offered to receive members of his household carrying a passport issued by him.[249] Despite these precautions, plague entered the town and was especially severe. The flight of so many wealthy townspeople meant that the municipal council were unable to organise an adequate guard for

---

[246] AM Amiens AA 60.

[247] At Douai in September 1667, the municipal deliberations note the arrival of the plague and of soldiers at the same time, while a poorly buried body of a soldier who had died from plague was believed to be the origin of the plague which struck Lyon over the winter of 1628–9: AM Douai, BB 16, fol. 32v; Lucenet, *Grandes pestes*, p. 110.

[248] Beaurepaire, 'Peste à Rouen', p. 217.

[249] AM Narbonne BB 5, fol. 390. See also: BB5, fol. 397.

the walls. Threats to levy heavy fines on the absent if they did not return immediately had little effect. This situation was doubly concerning both because it was a period of civil war and there were enemy soldiers in the region and because they were unable to fully control access to the town. Accordingly, they appealed to Joyeuse to send soldiers to support them, in response to which the duke dispatched fifty of his own men and declared that he would help the town in any way he could.[250] Narbonne's *consuls* continued to call for military aid during severe outbreaks of plague. In 1631, the governor again provided soldiers to serve as the council's guard and help them enforce anti-plague measures.[251] When the plague struck the city for the final time in the early 1650s, it was especially severe and the town emptied. During a council meeting in September 1652, one of the *consuls* commented 'on the deplorable state of the town, which the violence of contagious disease has rendered deserted, having only about 300 inhabitants at present'.[252] The *consuls* again sought the support of soldiers, both to defend Narbonne from attack in the absence of so many townspeople and to help them execute their functions and police the town. With so many houses empty, the conditions were ideal for widespread criminality.[253]

The capacity to employ soldiers could be built into the authority granted to towns during plague outbreaks. Amongst the plague powers given to the *consuls* at Aix-en-Provence in 1587 was the ability to raise a company of footmen to act as a police force.[254] To this end, towns could employ men to maintain order. At Saint-Flour in 1628, the town council employed one sieur Gibaudan and gave him full police powers to maintain order in the town, which he did well despite being 'in peril of his life' so much so that the town in the following year granted him an annual pension.[255] Soldiers supported municipal councils across France during the sixteenth and seventeenth centuries, principally because urban rulers struggled to find enough men to maintain order. When plague struck Limoges in 1631, due to 'all the inhabitants leaving and abandoning the city without leaving the means to provide for its security, custody and conservation', the town council appealed to the governor of Limousin to send them 'a company composed of such a number of soldiers as will be advised, under the charge of a faithful captain' to maintain order in the town and prevent criminality.[256] In a letter to Louis XIII, Villefranche-en-Rouergue's *consuls* explained how they had employed thirty soldiers 'to protect the city', although most of them had died and they were now seeking royal

---

[250] AM Narbonne BB 5, fols. 436, 440v, 450, 453v–456v.   [251] AM Narbonne BB 18, fol. 61v.
[252] AM Narbonne BB 23, fol. 240.   [253] AM Narbonne BB 23, fols. 241v–242r.
[254] AM Aix-en-Provence CC 875, fol. 177v.   [255] Boudet and Grand, *Documents inédits*, p. 94.
[256] Ruben (ed.), *Registres consulaires*, vol. III, pp. 275, 277.

support.[257] The *consuls* were probably keen to emphasise that they were doing all they could to enforce the strict application of plague ordinances, which the Crown was increasingly demanding. There were other advantages to employing soldiers who, as non-natives, had no local ties which might have prevented them from only laxly enforcing plague measures.

Soldiers continued to be employed in towns through to the eighteenth century, though they were increasing drafted by the Crown. Yet municipal governments continued to welcome the presence of soldiers to help them keep order and enforce plague regulations. The sending of the military was not an abrogation of municipal power. Jean-Baptiste Bertrand, the municipal physician at Marseille in 1720, recorded that 'the king, informed of our deplorable situation, was pleased to appoint Mons. le Chevalier de Langeron, *chef d'es-cadre* of the galleys, temporary commandment of the city and territory of Marseilles; upon which office he entered on 12th September, to the great satisfactions of the *échevins*, who were charged with notifying to him his appointment'.[258] As plague took hold at Arles in the summer of 1721, the introduction of strict quarantine led to disturbances from the population. To restore order and enforce the anti-plague regulations, the *intendant* introduced a company of soldiers into the town in June 1721 to support the *consuls*:

> you need armed authority in a town to prevent looting. In such an unfortunate time, the consuls have enough to do in providing for the necessities of the people and the sicknesses; the police offices are deserted as soon as the evil [i.e. the plague] becomes violent, and in Arles where so many people have sacrificed themselves to serve the public, the police office was only made up of a few people.[259]

As we have seen, there was nothing new about the use of soldiers to combat plague in the 1720s as this had been widespread over the previous two centuries, though it was now the Crown which dispatched regiments of royal soldiers to help the towns.

The Monarch

Over the course of the sixteenth and seventeenth centuries, French monarchs took an increasing interest in the impact of plague on their kingdom. Before the mid-sixteenth century, monarchs tended to only intervene in the local manage-ment of plague when it affected them directly.[260] When Charles VIII planned to

---

[257] Cited in : Mouysset, 'Peste de 1628', p. 335.   [258] Bertrand, *Plague at Marseilles*, p. 181.

[259] Cited in : Caylux, *Arles et la peste*, pp. 88–9.

[260] Though they could also issue tax remissions to towns badly affected by the plague. Charles VI, for instance, reduced the *feux* payment due by Albi in consideration of the impact of plague and war on the town: AD Tarn 4 EDT CC 83, no. 25, EDT CC 100, no. 1.

visit Compiègne in 1493, his *maréchal des logis* wrote to the town council to know if there was any danger from the 'disease of plague'. The town council sent him a detailed report of plague deaths in the region, which the *maréchal* verified by seeking the opinion of the town's physicians and surgeons.[261] In July 1475, when there was an epidemic at Beauvais, Jacques Coitier, the chief physician to Louis XI, wrote to the town council instructing them to light bonfires day and night.[262] While French monarchs were peripatetic, they had a particular interest in Paris as the capital of the kingdom. In 1510, Louis XII sent orders to the municipal council of Paris from Blois forbidding any person from leaving the capital in case they contracted plague and returned to spread it. He claimed to be acting for the protection of his pregnant daughter, Claude, who was then in Paris.[263] Yet the measures for Paris could also carry a wider resonance. In 1533, Francis I had the *parlement* of Paris convene to issue ordinances 'concerning the police of the town and suburbs of Paris to avoid the danger of plague', which were implemented in the capital over the following two centuries.[264] As we shall see, royal initiatives taken for Paris in matters of plague prevention became a model for other towns and cities.

Sixteenth-century French monarchs tended to follow their medieval predecessors in acting to reduce the economic impact of plague upon urban communities. As well as seeking to protect his family's health, Louis XII granted tax reductions to communities badly affected by plague.[265] A range of plague-related issues came to the king and his council during this period, as we see when we examine the acts of Henry II (reigned 1547–59). In 1554, Henry II ordered his seneschals in Nantes to ensure that a merchant was reimbursed for the money he had loaned the town council to pay for plague relief, sums which the municipal council had been unable to recover because of the flight of the wealthy from the town.[266] The following year, he granted the *parlement* of Bordeaux permission to hold its sittings outside the city due to the presence of plague.[267] Towns seeking help from the king to alleviate the effects of the plague could first bring their case to the local royal officials, as this lent more weight to a request. During the plague which struck Nîmes in 1580, the town council appealed to Jean de Montcal, *président* and *lieutenant-général* of the *sénéchaussée* of Beaucaire and Nîmes, to ask Henry III for a tax remission on their behalf.[268] While this type of involvement was largely passive on the part of

---

[261] AM Compiègne BB/COM 13, fol. 59.   [262] Rose, *Inventaire sommaire, Beauvais*, p. 13.

[263] Bonnardot (ed.), *Registres des délibérations, Paris, 1499–1526*, pp. 161–2. See also for Louis XII's visit to Lyon with his family in 1509: AM Lyon AA 151.

[264] *Ordonnances* (1571), pp. 1061–4.   [265] BNF Français 5093, fols. 182–183v.

[266] AN Actes de Henri II 1554–01–23/4   [267] AN Actes de Henri II 1555–08–23/3

[268] BNF Français 5286, fols. 157–158v.

the monarchy – in that communities took the initiative to approach him – nonetheless these actions provided the king with a greater sense of the sanitary state of his kingdom. To ascertain whether a request for tax reduction during plague was legitimate, the monarch and his officers had to be able to determine how the request responded to the reality of the situation. For instance, as part of a tax-reduction case relating to the diocese of Angers in 1537, Francis I was able to note that plague was then present in only one village in the diocese (Trêves-Cunault).[269]

During the second half of the sixteenth century, French monarchs began to take a more active role in intervening in management of plague. We find a growing awareness of plague protection on the part of the monarchy during the reigns of the last Valois monarchs, Charles IX and Henry III. Where first the city council, then the *parlement* had issued the plague regulations at Paris, during the outbreak of the 1580s Henry III issued the list of plague ordinances.[270] Charles IX sought to prevent plague entering the kingdom and he issued instructions to frontier towns such as Metz to take precautions when he learned of plague outbreaks in foreign states.[271] He also looked to the sea frontiers of the kingdom. In 1571, he issued letters patent and the sum of 5,000 *livres* to Nantes for the building of a plague hospital, as the 'town and suburbs being maritime are very susceptible to plague and contagion'.[272] Charles also used the tours he made of his kingdom to learn about the impact of plague, as well as issuing significant tax reductions to places that were suffering severe outbreaks.[273]

It is likely that the work of Ambrose Paré, the surgeon for four successive kings in the second half of the sixteenth century (Henry II, Francis II, Charles IX and Henry III), who wrote a highly influential treatise on plague in 1568, played an important role in increasing the monarchy's interest in controlling the disease.[274] In addition, there was an expansion in both the number of royal physicians and the extent of their authority. Where Louis XII at the beginning of the sixteenth century had five royal physicians, Henry IV had thirty-seven by the early seventeenth century.[275] Henry IV also sought to more firmly integrate medical professionals into the operation of state power in France, including ruling that physicians were to be employed for the first time to make reports in legal cases. To this end, he gave his principal physician the right to name in

---

[269] Marichal (ed.), *Ordonnances, François Ier. Tome VIII*, p. 127.

[270] 'Ordre et reiglement que le Roy veult et ordonne à [René] de Villequier, Gouverneur de Paris, faire garder et observer par les prévost des marchans et eschevins' of Paris : BNF Français 16744, fols. 215–66.

[271] Verronnais, *Inventaire sommaire, Metz*, p. 75.   [272] AM Nantes AA 5.

[273] See, for instance : AD Somme I B 1, fol. 133v ; BNF 3943, no. 76.

[274] Paré, *Traicté de la peste*.   [275] Robert, 'Premier Médicin du Roi', p. 374.

every town two medical professionals (typically a physician and a surgeon) to prepare reports on all cases involving wounding or murder.[276] As we shall see, it was also Henry IV who began to make widespread use of royal physicians to advise municipal councils on the medical response to plague.

Certainly, Henry IV, the first Bourbon monarch, took greater personal involvement in the directing of plague measures than any previous French king. In many ways, he set the plague policy which subsequent Bourbon monarchs were to follow to the eighteenth century. These were based around three key principles: (1) strict enforcement of plague ordinances, especially those based around quarantine; (2) the use of large plague hospitals which followed the latest medical ideas and could accommodate great numbers of people; (3) the use of royal physicians to determine the best treatments and to advise towns. Already by the late 1590s, he was instructing towns in the northeast to take stricter measures with the plague than they had been doing. In 1604, he sent the master surgeon and expert bleeder of plague victims, Théodore de Béthune, to Amiens where there was a bad outbreak of plague.[277] Three years later, he ordered the construction of the Saint-Louis plague hospital just outside of Paris. While this represented the monarchy's ongoing concern with the capital, it was a proactive measure that would have national ramifications. This monumental institution provided the template for a new generation of plague hospitals, especially those built across northern France. During the seventeenth century, what happened at Paris was increasingly copied by other towns. At Nevers in 1670, for instance, the town council ruled that the streets of the town were to be cleaned 'like the city of Paris'.[278]

Much of the efforts at exporting the Parisian model and standardising plague responses across France occurred under Louis XIII, who took an active interest in the response to the major plague of the 1630s. His efforts represent an important stage in the monarch trying to oversee a national response to plague. Louis had royal officials in the provinces send him news of the sanitary state of their areas and advise him about what measures were being taken to combat the disease. The royal council assumed the character of a national health board in the 1630s when the king, advised by his personal physicians and surgeons, took decisions on matters relating to plague and had them applied in the localities. On 4 September 1636, for example, the vicomte de Brigueil, governor of Compiègne, which had just been infected with plague, received letters from Louis XIII requesting information about the number of infected houses. The governor then enforced the royal plague policy of Louis XIII and his council,

---

[276] Brittain, 'Origins of Legal Medicine', p. 25.   [277] AM Amiens GG 1118.

[278] Boutillier, *Inventaire sommaire, Nevers*, p. 8.

which was to remove all infected people, along with those who were suspected of infection, to the extramural plague hospital, as well as to expel all those who had come to the town seeking refuge (in other words, the foreign poor).[279] At Troyes, François de Rochèchouart, the royal *indendant* sent to the town in 1633, instructed the city's health board that any infected found 'wondering and communicating with the other inhabitants [were] to be shot without any trial'.[280] As we see, basic aspects of martial law were being applied almost a century before the plague of Provence.

Louis XIII was particularly concerned about instances where municipal councils were failing to apply the anti-plague measures rigorously. While we have read about the actions of Chaulnes at Amiens in the 1630s, it was the monarch who took personal oversight of events in the city and directed the governor in how to act in response to the townspeople's actions against Henry Le Cointe, the royal-approved *aireur*.[281] During a meeting of the royal council, Louis's chief physician spoke of 'the sickness of Amiens, that they were bad inhabitants and bad servants of the king ... with the intention of entirely losing the city'. As a result of this disobedience, the town council were instructed to keep the doctors in Paris apprised of the situation in Amiens. The king, 'knowing that the disorder in the city comes from some of your body who must be declared disturbers of the public peace', summoned the leader of this group to Paris to appear before him and his council within ten days. The monarch was now acting as the ultimate guarantor of the health of the kingdom. As the governor declared, their actions were 'prejudicial to the service of the king'.[282] Indeed, in 1635, Louis XIII's *conseil privé*, the innermost of the royal councils, issued an order that a new commission consisting of twelve members of the royal council was to oversee the implementation of anti-plague measures in the city.[283]

Although it was rare for the Crown to act so strongly in directing municipal actions, the dispatch of royal doctors from Paris or the court to oversee the implementation of anti-plague measures in the provinces was becoming more common during the seventeenth century. For instance, the royal physician, Inard, sent to Dieppe during the plague of the late 1660s, brought 'precautions against the plague' and police regulations to enforce.[284] In the 1660s, Louis XIV employed Léon Augustin Déchaussée 'to cure people attacked by the contagion' and his methods were seen as highly successful, so much so that his *Parfums et remèdes contre la peste* was republished in 1720 for use during the plague of Provence.[285] Déchaussée was part of a cadre of men – which included Le Cointe and Inard – coming to prominence because of their success

[279] Marsy, 'Défense de Compiègne', p. 57.   [280] Boutiot, *Pestes de Troyes*, p. 44.
[281] AM Amiens GG 1124.   [282] AM Amiens AA 60.   [283] AM Amiens GG 1124.
[284] BNF Clairambault 286, fols. 193–4.   [285] *Parfums et remèdes* (1720).

in implementing methods approved by the king against the plague. In his 1669 letter to Dieppe, Louis XIV ordered the town council 'very expressly to follow punctually the advice [of] Sieur Ivard, a physician very experienced in this disease'.[286] Beyond the widespread use of these approved medical treatments, the plague of 1667–70 saw further involvement from the Crown in the management of the disease.

Colbert, the *Intendants* and the Plague of 1667–70

While Louis XIV continued his father's policy of taking an active role in plague outbreaks, it was Jean-Baptiste Colbert, his principal minister of state, who oversaw the implementation and coordination of anti-plague measures in the late 1660s. During this plague, Colbert positioned himself at the centre of the response to the plague and enforced the policy which had been developed by the Crown from the reign of Henry IV. He continued to support urban governments by giving them the powers to enforce measures, including the right to use the death penalty (which many towns did not possess) as part of his *Ordres à observer pour empescher que la peste ne se communicque hors les lieux infectez*.[287] He also maintained the Bourbon policy of sending royal physicians and medical staff to affected towns to oversee the treatment of the infected.[288]

Like Louis XIII's actions in the 1630s, Colbert requested regular written reports from local officials about the health of their areas and what measures town councils were implementing to combat the plague. For instance, Nicolas Nacquart, *lieutenant-général de l'amirauté* of Dunkirk, wrote regularly to Colbert about the effort urban governments were taking against plague in the region. He reported that the response at Gravelines in August 1666 was disorderly, by which he meant that the town council were allowing the infected to remain at home rather than go to the plague hospital. Nacquart ruled that regardless of status or privilege all were to be sent to the plague hospital, which was a longstanding Bourbon policy. He took charge of the situation and extended the building so that it could accommodate more people, both townspeople and soldiers.[289] The initial response at Gravelines probably represents the ongoing preference for a less stringent type of quarantine in the north, which we saw in 1630s. By sending Nacquart to take control of the situation, Colbert was acting in a similar way to how Louis XIII had responded to the situation at Amiens thirty years earlier.

---

[286] Guibert, *Dieppe*, vol. II, p. 39.   [287] *Ordres à observer* (1668).
[288] Depping (ed.), *Correspondence, Louis XIV*, vol. I, pp. 798–9, 802–3.
[289] Depping (ed.), *Correspondence, Louis XIV*, vol. I, pp. 796–7.

Colbert issued instructions to affected towns, directing municipal governments to prevent entry to goods coming from infected places and to build quarantine centres. His orders complemented those coming from the *parlement* of Paris and royal officers of the *bailliages*, who helped municipal government by issuing regulations controlling the movements of people from rural areas.[290] In the spring of 1669, the *parlement* of Rouen issued an instruction forbidding the holding of the market at Torcy, which lay just outside Rouen, probably on the basis of a report by a delegation from Rouen's health board, which inspected Torcy and other contaminated parishes.[291] While prohibiting the fair, the *parlement* supported the population of Torcy by organising grain to be distributed amongst its poor.[292] Yet Colbert was principally concerned about big cities such as Amiens, Dieppe and Rouen. As soon as the disease reached Rouen, he ordered detailed reports about the specific number of infected in the city.[293] While focusing on the northeast, Colbert looked across the entire kingdom, for instance by having Marseille send him a printed model health certificate, presumably to be used in the northeast.[294]

Colbert was aware of the financial pressure which towns were under and he acted to help them. First, he made grants and provided tax remissions. In September 1668, for instance, the mayor of La Fère appealed to him to authorise the levying of a plague tax on the population.[295] The following month, Colbert granted Dieppe the right to collect money raised on the town's tax farms to pay for plague relief.[296] Second, he introduced plague-control measures designed to allow controlled trade to continue. As Colbert was then seeking to implement a form of nationalistic mercantilism by which the state actively intervened to encourage domestic commerce, these plague policies were in line with his wider economic vision for France.[297] He saw the commercial devastation plague caused, which ultimately damaged state revenues through tax reductions. The president of the *parlement* of Normandy informed him in September 1668 that Normandy 'will fall into the final misery' because the fairs were not running and commerce had ceased due to the plague, so that they could not pay the required *taille* (the main direct tax in France).[298] In 1669, Rouen sought a reduction of 20,000 *livres* for its contribution to the *taille*, while Alençon (at which there

---

[290] AM Amiens GG 1130.   [291] BNF Mélanges Colbert 151bis, fols. 980–7.

[292] BNF Mélanges Colbert 152, fols. 116–21, 153, fols. 264–74, 406–70.

[293] BNF Mélanges Colbert 153, fols. 264–74, 406–70.

[294] BNF Mélanges Colbert 149, fol. 718.

[295] Clément (ed.), *Lettres, Colbert*, vol. II, 443; Depping (ed.), *Correspondence, Louis XIV*, vol. I, pp. 798–9.

[296] Depping (ed.), *Correspondence, Louis XIV*, vol. I, pp. 798–9, 802–3.

[297] Richardt, *Colbertisme*.   [298] BNF Mélanges Colbert 148bis, fol. 619.

were 'more beggars than in any city in the kingdom') had its payment reduced by 29,000 *livres* and Caen by 120,000 *livres*.[299]

Given that this was a time of war with Spain (pursued over expansionist policies in the Low Countries to support Colbert's economic vision), it was important to have the economies of the urban belt of the northeast functioning as far as possible. To this end, instead of using blanket trade embargos, he allowed commerce to continue by establishing *évents* outside of the cities. These were locations where suspect goods were disinfected by exposure to the wind or with perfumes before being brought into towns for sale (the plague sick could also be brought here if the plague hospital was full). At Amiens, the *évent* was held at the village of Dury, while other major urban centres such as Dieppe and Rouen held similar *évents* at nearby villages.[300] Again, rural populations suffered to maintain the health of the towns. In this way, Colbert was seeking to use plague-control measures to allow some commerce to continue rather than have economic paralysis. The *intendant* of Amiens called the *évents* 'the most sovereign of all remedies'.[301] Yet they were a development of older practices which had been implemented by towns. At the beginning of the sixteenth century, Rouen had an *évent* at a farm outside of the city, where the goods and clothing of the plague infected were disinfected, which was still being used in the 1620s.[302] During the mid-sixteenth century, Lyon used the village of Chazay-d'Azergues to quarantine goods coming into the city.[303] Moreover, the *cordons sanitaire* Colbert used in the late 1660s were a continuation of urban practices, as towns set up their own sanitary cordons and regulated trade accordingly. When Troyes' rulers learned that plague was present in towns of Normandy and the Île-de-France in the 1620s, they set up a quarantine for goods at Saint-Martin-lès-Vignes, a village lying outside the town. Again in 1668, when plague hit Picardy, they set up their own sanitary cordon, which included placing thousands of people who had fled Amiens in extramural quarantine.[304]

If the use of *cordons sanitaire* and the disinfection of goods were not new, the plague of 1667–70 was the first time that the *intendants* coordinated such measures across a wide region. *Intendants* did not supplant the position of the *parlements*, which remained central to the management of the outbreak; rather, they complemented each other. While the *intendant* oversaw the implementation of anti-plague measures in 1660s, it was the *parlements* which applied or lifted general restrictions. Moreover, like the *parlements*, they frequently buttressed municipal authority. In September 1668, Amiens placed guards on each gate to

---

[299] Esmonin, *Taille en Normandie*, p. 72; BNF Mélanges Colbert 155, fol. 338.

[300] BNF Mélanges Colbert 153, fols. 471–9.   [301] AM Amiens BB 72, fol. 28.

[302] In 1537, the *parlement* confiscated land for this purpose: Fournée, *Normands*, p. 42.

[303] AM Lyon AA 137.   [304] Boutit, *Troyes*, p. 41.

prevent people from neighbouring villages from entering the uninfected city. The *intendant* strengthened this measure by limiting communication between Amiens and infected settlements, as well as sending men to each village to ensure that the inhabitants observed the plague regulations. They also formed the conduit through which financial relief from the Crown was sent to infected towns.[305] Following the cessation of plague, the *intendants* continued to provide financial support to towns to help them recover. At Douai, which was still reeling from the high costs of plague care, the *intendant* helped the town council reduce the sums that the governor was demanding of them for support of his troops in 1670.[306]

While there is little focused work on the *intendants* and epidemics, they became central to the management of both human and animal diseases in the eighteenth century. With the outbreak of plague in Provence in 1720–2, *intendants* across the kingdom once again supervised the implementation of local measures, including issuing plague ordinances, installing health boards and checking bills of health. The *intendants* passed on reports to the king about the situations in their jurisdictions, as the provincial governors had done in the previous century.[307] When rinderpest infected cattle populations across Europe in the eighteenth century, *intendants* began to use measures taken for plague (such as quarantining and travel restrictions) to prevent the spread of bovine disease. Furthermore, those situated near ports remained vigilant for the return of plague, which remained rife in the Baltic and the Mediterranean.[308] Yet the key strategy remained one of support for municipalities and towns continued to work closely with the *intendants* in the way that they had done with other provincial agents of the Crown.

***

During the sixteenth and seventeenth centuries, France developed a plague-relief system composed of multiple actors, each of whom used their own powers and authority. The institutional structures of plague management were adapted to accommodate new individuals and institutions, developments which reflect the growing complexity and sophistication of the early modern French state. The Crown and its agents supported the actions of town councils by both lending their authority to enforce measures and providing financial support, as well monitoring the situation to ensure that plague ordinances were being enforced rigorously at a local level. While the direct involvement of the monarchy increased steadily from the mid-sixteenth century, to some extent it was already there in the form of tax remissions. Furthermore, even before the involvement of the king, town

---

[305] See here: AM Amiens GG 1135–37.
[306] See for instance: AM Douai BB 7, fol. 178v; AM Amiens GG 1139, 1140; Parmentier, *Archives de Nevers*, vol. I, p. 215.
[307] AM Amiens GG 1139, 1140.   [308] Beaurepaire, 'Peste à Rouen', pp. 206–8, 221.

governments liked to invoke royal authority to help them enforce plague regulations, which were generally unpopular. In 1484, Bergerac's town council 'on
behalf of the king our lord and *messeigneurs* the consuls' ruled that anyone who
disobeyed plague regulations would have 'great penalties' imposed on them by
'*messeigneurs* the officers of the king our lord and *messeigneurs* the consuls'.[309]
In the politically fragmented realm of late medieval France, French kings were
only one source of authority and municipal councils also appealed to other
political authorities for their support in enforcing plague regulations. In
September 1485, the duke of Brittany ordered the physician Artur Savaton to
take up the role of plague surgeon at Nantes, which was then infected by the
plague.[310] As royal power grew, the monarch and his agents in the provinces
(*parlements*, governors or *intendants*) began to take over this role. In this way, the
growing involvement of the Crown was a symbol of its increased power and
authority. It may also have been for this reason why kings began to take a stronger
interest in plague during the Wars of Religion in the second half of the sixteenth
century, when there were strong challenges to royal authority. It was at the very
moment Henry IV secured his throne in the mid-1590s that he began instructing
towns, many of whom had previously been opposed to him, to strongly implement their plague regulations. Although this was a mark of growing royal power,
the Crown did not supplant municipal councils who remained vital to the system,
which for the most part was marked by cooperation and support.

5 Epilogue

Rather than see the plague of Provence as representing the development of a new
system of 'modern' disease control, we should see it as the fullest expression of
a system which had been developing over the previous two or more centuries. The
fundamental aspects of the approach used at Provence in the 1720s were already
in place by the early seventeenth century and had antecedents going back into the
fifteenth century. By means of this polycentric system, municipal councils, with
the support of royal authorities in the provinces, as well as other urban groups
such as the clergy, implemented plague regulations. The direct involvement of the
monarchy in plague-relief schemes increased during the later sixteenth century
and by the plague of the 1630s the monarch and his council monitored these
developments closer than ever before. The development of a national *Conseil de
santé* in 1721 was certainly an important step in the development of public health,
though it represents a further specialisation in government offices rather than the
opening of a new area of policy, as the royal council was effectively already filling
this function by the 1630s. As we saw in Section 3, Louis XIII and his chief

---

[309] Charrier (ed.), *Registres de l'hôtel de ville*, vol. I, p. 336.   [310] AM Nantes CC 102.

ministers received reports about the sanitary state of affected towns and responded accordingly. The king worked with the advice of his royal physicians, whom he dispatched to stricken areas to advise urban governments. Although the king preferred to support towns, Louis was prepared to send in the military to enforce regulations (though, as we saw, soldiers assisted municipal councils during plague outbreaks long before the 1720s).

The king also took decisions regarding the medical infrastructure to be used in towns, particularly with regard to plague hospitals which were to follow the royal design laid down by Henry IV in 1607. This was combined with extensive targeted financial relief from the Crown to support local plague-relief efforts. There was a regional aspect to it in that royal control over plague management was traditionally stronger in the north where it concentrated its efforts. In a large part this was probably because under the Bourbon monarchs the great centralising initiatives came from Paris, though in terms of plague the south also had a longer tradition of implementing the strict Italian-style quarantine methods which the Bourbon monarchy favoured but which we saw found still some resistance amongst urban elites of the north even as late as the 1660s.[311] The fundamental way in which Provence was different to what had come before was that the monarchy under Louis XV was stronger that it had been even during the first half of Louis XIV's reign. It was the capacity for the monarchy to realise its ambitions rather than policies themselves which were notable in the 1720s, though it is still far from being anywhere near as omnipotent as the 'surveillance system' Foucault outlined in his discussion of plague-control measures in early modern France.[312]

This Element has sought to provide a broad sketch of the contours which led to the development of a comprehensive anti-plague system in France (one that would later be exported to North Africa and the Middle East as France expanded its colonial influence from 1798). The different elements which comprise this system are all worthy of further detailed study, especially given the lack of work on the role of regional royal authorities. There is no focused study of the *intendants* and public health, though their importance in this area has been noted. The ten volumes of correspondence relating specifically to plague (now at the Bibliothèque Nationale de France) left by the *intendant* of Provence in the 1720s have not been well studied, despite the vast amount of research on the plague of Provence. The role of the *intendants* in the health of the kingdom was crucial in the eighteenth century not just for epidemics but also for epizootics, which have received little study for the early modern period.[313] While the link between the methods used against plague and other infectious disease such as

---

[311] For Bourbon centralisation, see: Collins, *State in Early Modern France*, p. 3.
[312] Foucault, *Discipline and Punish*, pp. 195–9.   [313] BNF NAF 22925–22934.

cholera has been noted (though still need to be discussed at length), there is very little on how they were transferred to animal diseases. Yet there are extensive comments on the link between human plague and bovine plague in the plague tracts produced about Provence in the 1720s, and we see measures such as sanitary cordons, quarantine and health passports being used during outbreaks of rinderpest in the eighteenth century. How far these methods, when used against human or animal populations, provoked similar responses to those encountered during plague merits attention. When the *suette* epidemic hit southern France in 1781–2, for instance, the measures introduced by the *intendants* led to widespread flight from cities.[314]

The plague of Provence was not the last time that the French would have to contend with plague. As Napoleon's army laid siege to Jaffa in 1798, the army's chief physician, René-Nicolas Desgenettes, describes how they encountered an outbreak of plague and introduced rigorous measures to combat the disease, including quarantine and specialist hospitals.[315] Al-Jabarti, an Arab eyewitness of French actions in 1798, commented how they 'exercise the greatest severity in the application of sanitary measures' which were not well received by the local population.[316] Certainly, it was French armies in North Africa in 1798 and 1830 which were the first to establish extensive quarantine schemes. With the expansion of French colonial rule in North Africa, these methods were imposed widely throughout the nineteenth century and beyond.[317] French influence in Africa and the Middle East was also crucial in seeing the adoption of quarantine methods in areas outside of direct French rule, such as the Ottoman reformers who adapted French methods to local conditions.[318] The pioneering French epidemiologist and physician to the Shah of Iran, Joseph Désiré Tholozan, in his account of the outbreaks of plague in Benghazi in 1858 and 1874, commented on the use of French methods of quarantine implemented by the physician Léonard Arnaud, then in the employment of the Ottoman sultan (the other French doctor who accompanied Arnaud died from the disease, probably making him one of the last French people to die from plague during the second pandemic).[319]

The plague of Provence was written about extensively at the time, which may have helped with the diffusion of these methods to other parts of Europe. The French *émigré*, Armand Emmanuel de Vigernot du Plessis, duke of Richelieu, who fled France for Russia after the Revolution, oversaw the municipal response

---

[314] Laffont, 'Ville et santé publique', p. 18.

[315] Desgenettes, *Histoire médicale de l'armée d'Orient*, p. 61.

[316] Cited in: Bulmuş, *Plague*, p. 99.

[317] The French continued to manage plague outbreaks in North Africa through the first half of the twentieth century: Poleykett, 'Spectacle of Disease'.

[318] Bulmuş, *Plague*, p. 98.   [319] Arnaud, *Peste de Benghazi*; Bulmuş, *Plague*, p. 138.

to the outbreak at Odessa in 1812, where upon the first signs of the disease he immediately enacted strict plague regulations, including quarantine, sanitary cordons and severe punishments (including shooting) for those who broke regulations, though, like Colbert 150 years earlier, he tried-to maintain the commercial life of the city.[320] In his report on the outbreak of plague at Malta in 1813–14, J. D. Tully, the surgeon attached to the British army based on the island, discussed the methods used at Marseille and noted how the British military authorities who governed the island implemented the rigorous enforcement of plague regulations based around quarantine and implemented severe punishments for those who broke the regulations.[321] French actions at Marseille were of great interest to men such as Tully who advocated the use of strict quarantine against infectious diseases, methods which were increasingly being challenged by anti-contagionists (such debates would continue during the third pandemic of plague).[322] In 1822, the French doubled down on the strict disease-control methods used against cholera and other infectious diseases, methods which were drawn from plague – and based around quarantine, military cordons and punishment – though the severity of the measures started to be reformed in the following decades, with anti-plague measures again forming a key part of the debate.[323]

Historians have long debated how far methods of containment and quarantine contributed to the disappearance of plague from mainland Europe during the eighteenth century. The debate about the effectiveness of such methods intersects with a debate about the characteristics of the disease. While the standard view remains that the disease of the second pandemic was the same as that of the third pandemic and that it was spread by fleas on rats, there are striking differences between the two pandemics. Historians such as Guido Alfani and Samuel Cohn have argued for human-to-human transmission, while a recent scientific study has also suggested that human ectoparasites, rather than rodent transmission, were a primary vector for the spread of the disease of the second pandemic.[324] Certainly, the cessation of outbreaks as a result of plague-control measures based around quarantine only makes sense if the disease was widely transmissible between people, rather than principally being a result of fleas on rodents.

For Lebrun, it was 'unquestionably' the 'central government policy' which had saved Paris and the wider kingdom from plague in the late 1660s and then again in

---

[320] Crousaz-Crétet, *Duc de Richelieu*, pp. 113–17; Robarts, *Migration and Disease*, pp. 148–9.

[321] Tully, *History of Plague*. See also: Chase-Levenson, *Yellow Flag*, p. 63.

[322] Echenberg, *Plague Ports*; Henderson, *Florence Under Siege*, pp. 5–7; DeLacy, *Contagionism*; Zuckerman, 'Plague and Contagionism'. See also: Lynteris, *Ethnographic Plague*.

[323] Ségur-Dupeyron, *Mission en Orient*; Martínez, 'International Sanitary Conferences'; Murard and Zylberman, 'Santé publique', p. 206–7.

[324] Alfani and Cohn, 'Nonantola 1630'; Alfani, 'Survival Analysis'; Dean, 'Human Ectoparasites'.

the 1720s, ultimately leading to the cessation of the disease in France.[325] Yet it is not immediately clear why this should be the case as the Crown both did little that was genuinely new and was slow to respond both in the 1660s and 1720s. Indeed, Junko Takeda writes that the plague of Provence was a 'failure of centralization' and that the Bourbon monarchy failed to contain the disease.[326] The plague of the 1660s spread through much of north-eastern France, while even the building of stone walls manned by armed soldiers failed to stop the plague from spreading to Avignon and the Comtat Venaissin in the 1720s. Yet if the sanitary cordons did completely prevent plague from spreading, they may have slowed the spread of the disease down and reduced the number of infected on the roads. The use of similar cordons in other parts of Europe – from those used in Italy in the 1650s to the military frontier the Habsburgs constructed against the Ottomans in the mid-eighteenth century – appears to have had similar effects.[327] However, until we better understand the characteristics of the disease and how it spread the role of such measures will continue to remain an area of debate. During the heights of the Covid-19 measures in the UK, the Supreme Court judge Jonathan Sumption, also a widely published medieval historian, saw the extensive quarantine measures employed by the government as unprecedented.[328] Yet as we have seen, these methods have a long history and extend back to the later Middle Ages. Rather, what arose during the Covid-19 pandemic was another form of two long debates, which have been taking place for centuries, about (1) the ability of political authorities, whether that be a city council or an absolutist monarchy, to impose restrictive measures on its people, and (2) the effectiveness of extensive quarantine in stopping the spread of disease. As such, a consideration of how political systems shape disease control and how effective the measures outlined in this Element are to the treatment of infectious diseases is an issue of ongoing importance.

---

[325] Lebrun, 'Intervention', p. 48.   [326] Takeda, *Crown and Commerce*, pp. 125, 128.
[327] Alfani and Murphy, 'Lethal Epidemics', 328–9. See also: Slack, 'Perceptions of Plague', pp. 152–3.
[328] For Sumption and COVID, see: Coggon, 'Values'.

Bibliography

Archives

1 Central Archives
Paris

Archives Nationales de France
Actes de Henri II 1554–01–23/1555–08–23/3
JJ 226, 235, 264

Bibliothèque Nationale de France
Clairambault 286
Dupuy 659
Français 3943, 5093, 5286, 9557, 16744
Mélanges Colbert 148bis, 149, 150, 151bis, 152, 153, 155
Moreau 806
Acquisitions Françaises 22925–22934

2 Archives Departmentales
Gers
1Edépôt Auch BB 5, 6

Hérault
284 EDT 26

Meurthe-et-Moselle
B 1027, B 1076, B 1081, B 1146, B 1147, B 1149, B 1151, B 1924, B 1581,
B 2133, B 2346, B 5149, B 5385, B 5451, B 5433, B 5714, B 6188, B 6210,
B 6592, B 6659, B 6693, B 6951, B 6757

Seine-Maritime
3E 1 Rouen AA 14, 18, 20

Somme
IB 1

Tarn
4 EDT AA 4
4 EDT CC 83, 100

Vaucluse
FRAD084_E Dépôt Avignon AA 16, 17, 18, 19, 20

3 Archives Municipales and Communales
Aix-en-Provence
AA 14
BB 100, 143
CC 390, 875

Amiens
AA 60
BB 9, 16, 63, 72
GG 1118, 1124, 1130, 1132, 1135, 1136, 1139–40

Auriol
BB 4, 9

Beaune
Carton 23, 27, 88

Cambrai
AA 26
BB 2

Compiègne
BB/COM 13
CC/COM 37

Douai
BB 2, 7
CC 1205, 1206, 1208, 1209

Grenoble
AA 23
BB 2, 5, 6, 8

Lyon
AA 48, 66, 67, 72–3, 112, 114, 118, 137, 141, 151, 156, 157
BB 55, 67
3GG 006, 013–024

Nantes
AA 5
CC 102

Narbonne
BB 1, 2, 5, 18, 23

Nice
GG 70/4/5/9/13/15

Printed Primary Sources

Affre, Henri, *Ville de Rodez: Inventaire sommaire des archives communales antérieures à 1790* (Rodez: E. Carrère, 1878).

Arnaud, Léonard, *Essai sur la peste de Benghazi en 1874* (Constantinople: Typographie et Lithographie Centrales, 1875).

Bell, Dean Philip (ed.), *Plague in the Early Modern World: A Documentary History* (Abingdon: Routledge, 2019).

Bérenger, Théophile (ed.), *Journal du maître d'hôtel de Mgr de Belsunce durant la peste de Marseille 1720–1722* (Paris: Marie de Victor Palmé, 1878).

Bertrand, Jean-Baptiste, *A Historical Relation of the Plague at Marseilles in the Year 1720*, trans. Anne Plumptre (London: J. Mawman, 1805).

Boisville, Dast Le Vacher de, *Inventaire sommaire des registres de la Jurade, 1520 à 1783*, 4 vols. (Bordeaux: G. Gounouilhou, 1896).

Bonnardot, François (ed.), *Registres des délibérations du bureau de la ville de Paris: Tome premier 1499–1526* (Paris: Imprimerie nationale, 1883).

Boutillier, François, *Ville de Nevers. Ville de Dijon. Inventaire sommaire des archives communales antérieures à 1790* (Nevers: J. Vincent, 1876).

Charrier, Georges (ed.), *Les Jurades de la ville de Bergerac tirées des registres de l'hôtel de ville, 1352–1589*, 2 vols. (Bergerac: Imprimerie générale de Sud-Ouest, 1892).

Chéreau, Achille (ed.), *Les ordonnances faictes et publiées à son de trompe par les carrefours de ceste ville de Paris pour éviter le danger de peste 1531* (Paris: Léon Willem, 1873).

Clément, Pierre (ed.), *Lettres, instructions et mémoires de Colbert*, 10 vols. (Paris: Imprimerie impériale, 1861–73).

Depping, Georges B. (ed.), *Correspondence administrative sous le regne de Louis XIV*, 4 vols. (Paris: Imprimerie nationale, 1850–5).

Desgenettes, René, *Histoire médicale de l'armée d'Orient par le médecin en chef* (Paris: Croullebois, 1802).

Les edicts et ordonnances des roys de France (Lyon: Michel Iove, 1571).

Essarts, Nicolas-Toussaint des, *Dictionnaire universel de police, historique, chronologique, géographique de jurisprudence civile, criminelle et de police*, 2 vols. (Paris: G. F. Quillau, 1786–90).

Garnier, Joseph (ed.), *Journal de Gabriel Breunot, conseiller au parlement de Dijon*, 3 vols. (Dijon: J. E. Rabutot, 1875).

Gouvenain, Louis de, *Ville de Dijon: Inventaire sommaire des archives communales antérieures à 1790*, 5 vols. (Dijon: F. Carré, 1867–1910).

Guérin, Paul (ed.), *Registres de délibérations du Bureau de la ville de Paris: Tome troisième, 1539–1552* (Paris: Imprimerie nationale, 1886).

Lérisse, Guillaume de, *Petit traité de la peste et des moyen de se preserver d'icelle* (Grenoble, 1597).

Marichal, Paul (ed.), *Ordonnances des rois de France: Règne de Francois Ier. Tome 8* (Paris: Imprimerie nationale, 1963).

Marsy, Comte de, 'Mesures prises pour la défense de Compiègne, juillet-septembre 1636', *Bulletin de la Société de l'histoire de Paris et de l'Ile-de-France* 7 (1880), 53–8.

Matton, Auguste, *Ville de Laon: Inventaire sommaire des archives communales antériures à 1790* (Laon: A. Cortilliot, 1885).

Ordres à observer pour empescher que la peste ne se communicque hors les lieux infectez (Paris: Frederic Léonard, 1668).

Paré, Ambroise, *Traicté de la peste, de la petite verolle & rougeolle: avec une brefve description de la lepre* (Paris: André Wechel, 1568).

Parfums et remèdes contre la peste don't s'est servi, avec tout le succès possible, le père Léon Augustin, Déchaussé de France, lequel a été employé par le roi pour guerir les personnes attaquées de la contagion qui régnait en plusieurs endroits du Roïaume en 1656, 1667, 1668 et 1669, avec la manière de parfumer les maisons pour les preserver de l'air infecté (Paris: Louis-Denis Delatour & Pierre Simon, 1720).

Parmentier, Charles A., *Archives de Nevers ou inventaire historique des titres de la ville*, 2 vols. (Paris: Techener, 1842).

Rose, Renaud, *Ville de Beauvais: Inventaire sommaire des archives communales antérieures à 1790* (Beauvais: Imprimerie centrale administrative, 1887).

Ruben, Émile (ed.), *Registres consulaires de la ville de Limoges*, 3 vols. (Limoges: Chapouland, 1867–97).

Rules and orders to be observed by all justices of peace, mayors, bayliffs, and other officers, for prevention of the spreading of the infection of the plague: Published by His Majesties special command (London: John Bill and Christopher Barker, 1666).

Ségur-Dupeyron, Philippe de, *Mission en Orient: Rapport adressé à son excellence le ministre de l'agriculture* (Paris: Imprimerie royale, 1846).

Tuetey, Alexandre (ed.), *Registres des délibérations du bureau de la ville de Paris: Tome II, 1527–1539* (Paris: Imprimerie nationale, 1886).

Bibliography

Tully, John D., *The History of Plague as It Has Lately Appeared in the Islands of Malta, Gozo, Corfu, Cephalonia, &c.* (London: Longman, 1821).

Verronnais, Jules, *Ville de Metz: Inventaire sommaire des archives communales antérieures à 1790* (Metz: J. Verronnais, 1880).

Secondary Sources

Aberth, John, *Doctoring the Black Death: Medieval Europe's Medical Response to Plague* (London: Rowman and Littlefield, 2021).

Alexander, John T., *Bubonic Plague in Early Modern Russia: Public Health and Urban Disaster* (Oxford: Oxford University Press, 2003).

Alezais, Henri, *Le blocus de Marseille pendant la peste de 1720* (Valence, 1907).

Alfani, Guido, 'Plague in Seventeenth-Century Europe and the Decline of Italy: An Epidemiological Hypothesis', *European Review of Economic History*, 17 (2013), 408–30.

'A Survival Analysis of the Last Great European plagues: The Case of Nonantola (Northern Italy) in 1630', *Population Studies*, 73 (2019), 101–18.

Alfani, Guido and Samuel K. Cohn, 'Nonantola 1630: Anatomia di una pestilenza e meccanismi del contagio (con riflessioni a partire dalle epidemie Milanesi della prima età moderna)', *Popolazione e storia*, 8 (2007), 99–138.

Alfani, Guido, and Tommy E. Murphy, 'Plague and Lethal Epidemics in the Pre-Industrial World', *Journal of Economic History*, 77 (2017), 314–43.

Assereto, Giovanni, 'Polizia sanitaria e sviluppo delle istituzioni statali nella Repubblica di Genova', in Livio Antinielli and Stefano Levati (eds.), *Controllare il territorio: Norme, corpi et conflitti tra medioevo e prima Guerra Mondiale* (Soveria Mannelli, 2013), pp. 167–87.

Ballon, Hilary, *The Paris of Henri IV: Architecture and Urbanism* (Cambridge, Mass.: MIT Press, 1991).

Bamji, Alexandra, 'Health Passes, Print and Public Health in Early Modern Europe', *Social History of Medicine*, 32 (2019), 441–64.

Barbiche, Bernard, *Les institutions de la monarchie française à l'époque moderne* (Paris: PUF, 2012).

Beaurepaire, Charles de, 'La peste à Rouen, 1619-1623', in *Précis analytique des travaux de l'Académie de Rouen*, (1905–6), 177–246.

Beauvieux, Fleur, 'Expériences ordinaires de la peste. La société marseillaise en temps d'épidémie (1720–1724)', unpublished PhD thesis, École des Hautes Études en Sciences Sociales, 2 vols. (2017).

Beik, William, *Absolutism and Society in Seventeenth Century France: State Power and Provincial Aristocracy in Languedoc* (Cambridge: Cambridge University Press, 1985).

'The Absolutism of Louis XIV as Social Collaboration', *Past & Present*, 188 (2005), 195–224.

Belmas, 'Pouvoir politique et catastrophe sanitaire. La "publication" des épidémies de peste dans la France moderne', *Parlements: Revue d'histoire politique*, 25 (2017), 31–54.

Benedictow, Ole J., 'Biraben's List of the Plague Epidemics of the Second Plague Pandemic, 1346 – c.1690: Problems, Basis, Uses', *Annales de démographie historique*, 138 (2019), 213–23.

Bennassar, Bartolomé, *Recherches sur les grandes épidémies dans le nord de l'Espagne à la fin du XVIe siècle* (Paris: SEVPEN, 1969).

Bercé, Yves-Marie, *Croquants et nu-pieds. Les soulèvements paysans en France du XVI au XIXe siècle* (Paris: Gallimard, 1991).

Bertrand, Régis, *Henri de Belsunce (1670–1755): l'évêque de la peste de Marseille* (Marseille: Gaussen, 2020).

Biraben, Jean-Noël, *Les hommes et la peste en France et dans les pays européens et méditerranéens*, 2 vols. (Paris: Mouton, 1976).

Bollet, Claude, 'A propos du traitement de la peste en 1720 à Marseille', unpublished PhD thesis, Université de Marseille (1983).

Bouchot, L., 'La peste de Lorraine de 1630 à 1636. La depopulation dans la prévôté de Gondreville', *Le Pays Lorraine*, (1927), 145–59.

Boudet, Marcellin, and Roger Grand, *Documents inédits sur les grandes épidémies: Étude historique sur les épidémies de peste en Haute-Auvergne (XIVe-XVIIIe siècles)* (Paris: Picard, 1902).

Bourru, Henri, *Des épidémies qui régnèrent à Rochefort en 1694* (Paris: Octave Doin, 1882).

Boutiot, Théophile, *Recherches sur les anciennes pestes de Troyes* (Troyes: Bouquot, 1857).

Bowers, Kirsty Wilson, *Plague and Public Health in Early Modern Seville* (Woodbridge: Boydell, 2013).

Brittain, Robert P., 'The Origins of Legal Medicine in France: Henri IV and Louis XIV', *Medico-Legal Journal*, 35 (1967), 25–8.

Bruni, René, *Le pays d'Apt malade de la peste* (Aix-en-Provence: Édisud, 1980).

Bulmuş, Birsen, *Plagues, Quarantines and Geopolitics in the Ottoman Empire* (Edinburgh: Edinburgh University Press, 2012).

Buti, Gilbert, *Colère de Dieu, mémoire de hommes. La peste en Provence 1720–2020* (Paris : Éditions du cerf, 2020).

La peste à La Valette. La peste au village, 1720–1721 (Paris: Stendhal, 1998).

Canard, Jean, *Les pestes en Beaujolais, Forez, Jarez, Lyonnais du XIVème au XVIIIème* (Pradines: Canard, 1979).

Carmichael, Ann J., 'Contagion Theory and Contagion Practice in Fifteenth Century Milan', *Renaissance Quarterly*, 44 (1991), 213–56.

'Plague Legislation in the Italian Renaissance', *Bulletin in the History of Medicine*, 57 (1983), 508–25.

Plague and the Poor in Renaissance Florence (Cambridge: Cambridge University Press, 1986).

Carrière, Charles et al., *Marseille, ville morte. La peste de 1720* (Paris: M. Garçon, 1968).

Cavallo, Sandra, *Charity and Power in Early Modern Italy: Benefactors and their Motives in Turin, 1541–1789* (Cambridge: Cambridge University Press, 1995).

Caylux, Odile, *Arles et la peste, 1720–1721* (Aix-en-Provence: Presses universitaires de Provence, 2009).

Chase-Levenson, Alex, *The Yellow Flag: Quarantine and the British Mediterranean World, 1780–1860* (Cambridge: Cambridge University Press, 2020).

Chauvet, Pierre, *La lutte contre la une épidémie au 18ᵉ siècle. La peste du Gévaudan* (Paris: Amédée Legrand, 1939).

Chavant, Ferdinand, *La peste à Grenoble, 1410–1643* (Lyon: Storck, 1903).

Cipolla, Carlo M., *Cristofano and the Plague: A Study in the History of Public Health in the Age of Galileo* (Berkeley: University of California Press, 1973).

Faith, Reason, and the Plague in Seventeenth Century Tuscany (New York: Norton, 1981).

Fighting the Plague in Seventeenth Century Italy (Madison: University of Wisconsin Press, 1981).

Public Health and the Medical Profession in the Renaissance (Cambridge: Cambridge University Press, 1976).

Coggon, John, 'Lord Sumption and the Values of Life, Liberty and Security: Before and Since the COVID-19 Outbreak', *Journal of Medical Ethics*, 48 (2022), 779–84.

Cohn, Samuel K., *Cultures of Plague: Medical Thinking at the End of the Renaissance* (Oxford: Oxford University Press, 2009).

'Epidemiology of the Black Death and Successive Waves of Plague', *Medical History*, 52 (2008), 74–100.

Collins, James B., *The State in Early Modern France* (Cambridge: Cambridge University Press, 1995).

Columbus, Aaron, '"To Be Had for a Pesthouse for the Use of This Parish": Plague Pesthouses in Early Stuart London, c. 1600–1650', *Urban History* (2022).

Cook, Alexandra Parma, and Noble David Cook, *The Plague Files: Crisis Management in Sixteenth-Century Seville* (Baton Rouge: Louisiana State University Press, 2009).

Coomans, Janna, *Community, Urban Health and Environment in the Late Medieval Low Countries* (Cambridge: Cambridge University Press, 2021).

Coste, Joël, *Represéntations et comportements en temps d'épidémie dans la littérature imprimée de peste, 1490–1725* (Paris: Champion, 2007).

Coste, Laurent, 'Bordeaux et la peste dans la première motié du XVIIe siècle', *Annales du Midi*, 110 (1998), 457–80.

Crawshaw, Jane L. Stevens, 'The Beasts of Burial: *Pizzigamorti* and Public Health for the Plague in Early Modern Venice', *Social History of Medicine*, 24 (2011), 570–87.

'The Invention of Quarantine', in Carole Rawcliffe and Linda Clark (eds.), *The Fifteenth Century XII: Society in an Age of Plague* (Woodbridge, 2013), pp. 161–74.

Plague Hospitals: Public Health for the City in Early Modern Venice (Abingdon: Routledge, 2012).

Crousaz-Crétet, Léon de, *Le duc de Richelieu en Russie et en France, 1766–1822* (Paris: Firmin-Didot, 1897).

Curtis, Daniel. R., 'Was Plague an Exclusively Urban Phenomenon? Plague Mortality in the Seventeenth-Century Low Countries', *Journal of Interdisciplinary History*, 47 (2016), 139–70.

David, Henri, *La peste à Angers* (Paris, 1908).

Dean, Katharine R. et al., 'Human Ectoparasites and the Spread of Plague in Europe during the Second Pandemic', *Proceedings of the National Academy of Sciences*, 115 (2018), 1304–9.

DeLacy, Margaret, *The Germ of an Idea: Contagionism, Religion, and Society in Britain, 1660–1730* (Basingstoke: Palgrave Macmillan, 2016).

Demichel, Sébastien, *Risque et vigilance sanitaire. La côte méditerranéenne française face à la peste* (Berlin: De Gruyter, 2024).

Echenberg, Myron, *Plague Ports: The Global Urban Impact of Bubonic Plague, 1894–1901* (New York: New York University Press, 2007).

Eckert, Edward A., 'Boundary Formation and Diffusion of Plague: Swiss Epidemics from 1562 to 1669', *Annales de démographie historique*, (1978), 49–80.

The Structure of Plagues and Pestilences in Early Modern Europe: Central Europe, 1560–1640 (Basel: Karger, 1996).

El Hadj, Jamel, 'Les chirurgiens et l'organisation sanitaire contre la peste à Marseille, 17e-18e siècles', unpublished PhD thesis, École des Hautes Études en Sciences Sociales (2014).

Ermus, Cindy, *The Great Plague Scare of 1720: Disaster and Diplomacy in the Eighteenth-Century Atlantic World* (Cambridge: Cambridge University Press, 2023).

Esmonin, Edmond, *La taille en Normandie au temps de Colbert (1661–1683)* (Paris: Hachette, 1913).

Estadieu, Mathieu, *Notes chronologiques statistiques pour servir à l'histoire de la ville de Castres* (Montauban: Éditions de la Tour Gile, 1882).

Finley-Croswhite, S. Annette, *Henry IV and the Towns: The Pursuit of Legitimacy in French Urban Society, 1589–1610* (Cambridge: Cambridge University Press, 1999).

Fosseyeux, Marcel, 'Les premiers budgets municipaux d'assistance. La taxe au pauvres au XVIe siècle', *Revue d'histoire de l'Église en France*, 88 (1934), 407–32.

Foucault, Didier, and Sylvie Mouysset, 'Ordre et desordre de la peste dans le Midi Toulousian au XVIIe siècle', *Cahiers du centre d'étude d'histoire de la médicine*, 14 (2006), 15–38.

Foucault, Michel, *Discipline and Punish: The Birth of the Prison*, trans. Alan Sheridan (London: Penguin, 1975).

Fournée, Jean, *Les Normands face à la peste* (Flers: Le pays bas Normand, 1978).

Fusco, Idamaria, 'Governing the Emergency in 1690–92 Plague Epidemic in the Kingdom of Naples', *Annales de démographie historique*, 134 (2017), 95–123.

Gaffarel, Paul, and M. de Duranty, *La Peste de 1720 à Marseille et en France, d'après des documents inédits* (Paris: Perrin, 1911).

Geltner, Guy, *Roads to Health: Infrastructure and Urban Wellbeing in Later Medieval Italy* (Philadelphia: University of Pennsylvania Press, 2019).

'The Path to Pistoia: Urban Hygiene Before the Black Death', *Past & Present*, 246 (2020), 3–33.

Goury, Michel, *Un homme, une navire. La peste de 1720* (Marseille: Jeanne Laffitte, 2013).

Green, Monica, 'Out of the East (or North or South): A Response to Philip Slavin', *Past & Present*, 256 (2022), 283–323.

Grmek, Mirko D., 'Les vicissitudes des notions d'infection, de contagion et de germe dans la médicine antique', in Guy Sabbah (ed.), *Mémoires de Centre Jean Palerne, v. Texts médicaux: Latins Antiques* (Sainte-Etienne, 1984), pp. 53–70.

Guiart, Jules, *Histoire de la peste à Bourg-en-Bresse* (Lyon: A. Rey, 1933).

Guibert, Michel C., *Mémoires pour servir à l'histoire de la ville de Dieppe*, 2 vols. (Dieppe: A. Renaux, 1878).

Guilbert, Sylvette, 'À Châlons-sur-Marne au XVe siècle: un conseil municipal face aux épidémies', *Annales: E.S.C.*, 23 (1968), 1283–1300.

Harding, Robert, *Anatomy of a Power Elite: The Provincial Governors of Early Modern France* (New Haven: Yale University Press, 1979).

Henderson, John, 'Charity and Welfare in Early Modern Tuscany', in Jon Arrizabalaga et al. (eds.), *Health Care and Poor Relief in Counter-Reformation Europe* (London: Routledge, 1999), pp. 56–86.

Florence Under Siege: Surviving Plague in and Early Modern City (London: Yale University Press, 2019).

'The Invisible Enemy: Fighting the Plague in Early Modern Italy', *Centarus*, 62 (2020), 263–74.

'The Black Death in Florence: Medical and Communal Responses', in Steven Bassett (ed.), *Death in Towns: Urban Responses to the Dying and the Dead* (Leicester: Leicester University Press, 1992), pp. 136–50.

Hildesheimer, Françoise, *Le Bureau de Santé de Marseille sous l'ancien regime* (Marseille: Féderation historique de Provence, 1980).

Fléaux et société: de la grande peste au choléra. XIVe-XIXe siècle (Paris: Hachette, 1993).

La terreur et la pitié: l'Ancien régime à l'épreuve de la peste (Paris: Publisud, 1990).

Jillings, Karen, *An Urban History of Plague: Socio-Economic, Political and Medical Impacts on a Scottish Community, 1500–1650* (Abingdon: Routledge, 2018).

Jones, Colin, 'Plague and Its Metaphors in Early Modern France', *Representations*, 53 (1996), 97–127.

Jones, Colin, and Laurence Brockliss, *The Medical World of Early Modern France* (Oxford: Oxford University Press, 1997).

Jones, Lori, *Patterns of Plague: Changing Ideas and Plague in England and France, 1348–1750* (Montreal: McGill-Queen's University Press, 2022).

Kerkhoff, A. M. H. *Per imperatief plakkaat: Overheid en pestbestrijding in de Republiek der Zeven Verenigde Nederlanden* (Hilversum: Verloren, 2020).

Laffont, Jean-Luc, 'Ville et santé publique sous l'Ancien Régime', in Jean-Michel Goger and Nicolas Marty (eds.), *Cadre de vie, équipment, santé dans les sociétés méditerranées* (Perpignan: Presses universitaires de Perpignan, 2005), pp. 15–31.

Le Page, Henri, 'De la depopulation en Lorraine au XVIIe siècle', *Annuaire de la Meuthe*, (1851), 11–58.

Lebrun, François, 'L'intervention des autorites face aux crises de mortalite dans la France d'Ancien Regime', in Arthur E. Imhof (ed.), *Leib und Leben in*

Der Deschichte Der Neuzeit (Berlin: Duncker & Humbolt, 1983), pp. 39–52.

Lièvre, Auguste-François, *La misère et les épidémies à Angoulême aux XVIe et XVIIe siècles* (Angoulême: L. Coquemard, 1886).

Lucenet, M., *Les grandes pestes en France* (Paris: Aubier, 1985).

Lynteris, Christos, *Ethnographic Plague: Configuring Disease on the Chinese-Russian Frontier* (London: Palgrave, 2016).

MacKay, Ruth, *Life in a Time of Pestilence: The Great Castilian Plague of 1596–1601* (Cambridge: Cambridge University Press, 2019).

Magen, Adolphe, 'La ville d'Agen pendant l'épidémie de 1628 à 1631 d'après les registres consulaires', *Revue de Gascogne*, 10 (1860), 108–57.

Malpart, Maurice, *La peste à Amiens au XVIIe siècle: étude medico-historique* (Amiens: Imprimerie nouvelle, 1938).

Martínez, Francisco Javier, 'International or French? The Early International Sanitary Conferences and France's Struggle for Hegemony in the Mid-Nineteenth Century Mediterranean', *French History*, 30 (2016), 78–80.

Mousnier, Roland, *Fureurs paysannes: les paysans dans les révoltes du XVIIe siècle (France, Russie, Chine)* (Paris: Calmann-Lévy, 1967).

Mouysset, Sylvie, 'La peste de 1628 en Rouergue', *Annales du Midi*, 105 (1993), 329–48.

Murard, Lion, and Patrick Zylberman, 'Heurs et malheurs de la santé publique en France (1848–1945)', *Horizontes, Bragança Paulista*, 22 (2004), 205–18.

Murphy, Neil, 'Plague Hospitals and Poor Relief in Late Medieval and Early Modern France', *Social History*, 47 (2022), 349–71.

'Plague Hospitals, Poverty and the Provision of Medical Care in France, c.1450-c.1650', *Journal of Social History*, 55 (2022), 825–53.

Newman, Kira L. S., 'Shutt Up: Bubonic Plague and Quarantine in Early Modern England', *Journal of Social History*, 45 (2012), 809–34.

Noordegraaf, Leo, and Gerrit Valk, *De gave Gods: de pest in Holland vanaf de late middelleeuwen* (Bergen: Bert Bakker, 1988).

Nutton, Vivian, 'The Seeds of Disease: An Explanation of Contagion and Infection from the Greeks to the Renaissance', *Medical History*, 27 (1983), 1–34.

Palmer, Richard J., 'The Control of Plague in Venice and Northern Italy, 1348-1600', unpublished PhD thesis, University of Kent (1978).

Peris, Fernando Varela, 'El papel de la Junta Suprema de Sanidad en la política sanitaria Española del siglo XVIII', *Dynamis*, 18 (1998), 315–40.

Poleykett, Branwyn, 'Public Culture and the Spectacle of Disease in Rabat and Casablanca', in Lukas Engelmann et al. (eds.), *Plague and the City* (London, 2018), pp. 159–72.

Porchev, Boris, *Les soulèvements populaires en France de 1623 à 1648* (Paris: SEVPEN, 1963).

Praviel, Armand, *Belsunce et la peste de Marseille* (Paris: E. Ramlot, 1936).

Pullan, Brian, 'Plague and Perceptions of the Poor in Early Modern Italy', in Terence Ranger and Paul Slack (eds.), *Epidemics and Ideas: Essays on the Historical Perception of Pestilence* (Cambridge: Cambridge University Press, 1992), pp. 101–24.

Rawcliffe, Carole, *Urban Bodies: Communal Health in Late Medieval English Towns and Cities* (Woodbridge: Boydell, 2013).

Rawcliffe, Carole, and Claire Weeda (eds.), *Policing the Urban Environment in Premodern Europe* (Amsterdam: Amsterdam University Press, 2019).

Revel, Jacques, 'Autour d'une épidémie ancienne. La peste de 1666-1670', *Revue d'histoire moderne et contemporaine*, 17 (1970), 953–83.

Richardt, Aimé, *Colbert et le colbertisme* (Paris: Tallandier, 1997).

Robarts, Andrew, *Migration and Disease in the Black Sea Region: Ottoman–Russian Relations in the Late Eighteenth and Early Nineteenth Centuries* (London: Bloomsbury, 2016).

Robert, 'Le Premier Médicin du Roi', *Histoire des sciences médicales*, 32 (1998), 374–8.

Roger, Euan C., '"To Be Shut Up": New Evidence for the Development of Quarantine Regulations in Early-Tudor England', *Social History of Medicine*, 33 (2020), 1077–96.

Rolland, Eugène de. , and Denis Clouzet, *Dictionnaire illustré des communes du département du Rhône*, 2 vols. (Lyon: Dizain & Storck, 1901–2).

Rommes, Ronald, 'Plague in Northwestern Europe: The Dutch Experience, 1350-1670', *Popolazione e storia*, 16 (2015), 47–71.

Roosen, Joris, and Daniel R. Curtis, 'Dangers of Noncritical Use of Historical Plague Data', *Emerging Infectious Diseases*, 24 (2018), 103–10.

Roucaud, Josèph, *La Peste à Toulouse: des origines à dix-huitième siècle* (Toulouse: J. Marqueste, 1918).

Siena, Kevin, *Rotten Bodies: Class and Contagion in Eighteenth-Century Britain* (New Haven: Yale University Press, 2019).

Slack, Paul, *The Impact of Plague in Tudor and Stuart England* (Oxford University Press, 1985).

'Perceptions of Plague in Eighteenth-Century Europe', *Economic History Review*, 75 (2022), 138–56.

Slavin, Philip, 'Out of the West: Formation of a Plague Reservoir in South-Central Germany (1349–1356) and Its Implications', *Past & Present*, 252 (2021), 3–51.

Takeda, Junko Thérèse, *Between Crown and Commerce: Marseille and the Early Modern Mediterranean* (Baltimore: The Johns Hopkins University Press, 2011).

Tomić, Zlata Blažina, and Vesna Blažina, *Expelling the Plague: The Health Office and the Implementation of Quarantine in Dubrovnik, 1377–1533* (Montreal: McGill-Queen's University Press, 2015).

Trout, Andrew P., 'The Municipality of Paris Confronts the Plague of 1668', *Medical History*, 17 (1973), 418–23.

Udale, Charles, 'Evaluating Early Modern Lockdowns: Household Quarantine in Bristol, 1565–1604', *Economic History Review*, 76 (2023), 118–44.

'The Purpose of Pesthouses in Early Modern England' (unpublished paper, 2023).

Varlik, Nüket, *Plague and Empire in the Early Modern Mediterranean World: The Ottoman Experience, 1347–1600* (Cambridge: Cambridge University Press, 2015).

Vidal, Auguste, 'La peste d'Albi en 1630, 1631 & 1632', *Revue historique, scientifique et littéraire du département du Tarn*, (1890), 172–80.

Zuckerman, Arnold, 'Plague and Contagionism in Eighteenth-Century England: The Role of Richard Mead', *Bulletin of the History of Medicine*, 78 (2004), 273–308.

Cambridge Elements ≡

The Renaissance

John Henderson
Birkbeck, University of London, and Wolfson College, University of Cambridge

John Henderson is Emeritus Professor of Italian Renaissance History at Birkbeck, University of London, and Emeritus Fellow of Wolfson College, University of Cambridge. His recent publications include *Florence Under Siege: Surviving Plague in an Early Modern City* (2019), *Plague and the City*, edited with Lukas Engelmann and Christos Lynteris (2019), and *Representing Infirmity: Diseased Bodies in Renaissance Italy*, edited with Fredrika Jacobs and Jonathan K. Nelson (2021). He is also the author of *Piety and Charity in Late Medieval Florence* (1994); *The Great Pox: The French Disease in Renaissance Europe*, with Jon Arrizabalaga and Roger French (1997); and *The Renaissance Hospital: Healing the Body and Healing the Soul* (2006). Forthcoming publications include a Cambridge Element, *Representing and Experiencing the Great Pox in Renaissance Italy* (2023).

Jonathan K. Nelson
Syracuse University Florence

Jonathan K. Nelson teaches Italian Renaissance Art at Syracuse University Florence and is research associate at the Harvard Kennedy School. His books include *Filippino Lippi* (2004, with Patrizia Zambrano); *Leonardo e la reinvenzione della figura femminile* (2007), *The Patron's Payoff: Conspicuous Commissions in Italian Renaissance Art* (2008, with Richard J. Zeckhauser), *Filippino Lippi* (2022); and he co-edited *Representing Infirmity. Diseased Bodies in Renaissance Italy* (2021). He co-curated museum exhibitions dedicated to Michelangelo (2002), Botticelli and Filippino (2004), Robert Mapplethorpe (2009), and Marcello Guasti (2019), and two online exhibitions about Bernard Berenson (2012, 2015). Forthcoming publications include a Cambridge Element, *Risks in Renaissance Art: Production, Purchase, Reception* (2023).

Assistant Editor
Sarah McBryde, *Birkbeck, University of London*

Editorial Board

About the Series
Timely, concise, and authoritative, Elements in the Renaissance showcases cutting-edge scholarship by both new and established academics. Designed to introduce students, researchers, and general readers to key questions in current research, the volumes take multi-disciplinary and transnational approaches to explore the conceptual, material, and cultural frameworks that structured Renaissance experience.

Cambridge Elements ≡

The Renaissance

Elements in the Series

Printed in the United States
by Baker & Taylor Publisher Services